BEST-LOVED
RECIPES

Publications International, Ltd.

Recipes, text and photographs on pages 15, 16, 17, 19, 20, 21, 23, 25, 27, 33, 37, 39, 49, 51, 53, 54, 55, 67, 70, 71, 73, 75, 76, 79, 81, 83, 92, 93, 95, 97, 99, 107, 110, 113, 115, 116, 119, 121, 131, 132, 143, 147, 149, 162, 167, 169, 171, 173, 189, 191, 193, 195, 197, 199, 215, 217, 219, 239, 241, 243, 245, and 247 © 2011 The Quaker Oats Company. All other photographs © 2011 Publications International, Ltd.

Dole®—Trade-mark of Dole Food Company, Inc. Used under licence.

Quaker®, the Quaker Man, Tropicana Pure Premium®, Aunt Jemima®, Kretschmer®, Oatmeal Squares™, Life® and Crispy Minis® —Trade-marks of PepsiCo, Inc. and related companies. Used under licence.

Pictured on the front cover: Fruitful Morning Muesli *(page 34)*.
Pictured on the back cover: Cranberry Orange Bread *(page 46)*, Cuban Meatball Kabobs *(page 102)*. and Queen of Hearts Frozen Berry Tart *(page 157)*.

ISBN-13: 978-1-4508-3102-4
ISBN-10: 1-4508-3102-8

Library of Congress Control Number: 2011929898

Manufactured in China.

8 7 6 5 4 3 2 1

Microwave Cooking: Microwave ovens vary in wattage. Use the cooking times as guidelines, and check for doneness before adding more time.

Publications International, Ltd.

# CONTENTS

Enjoy the GOODNESS *of* OATS

Everywhere you look today, people are over-committed, over-tired, and overwhelmed. While we try to accomplish more and more on our endless to-do lists, we miss out on the good things in life.

However, there's hope. It's never too early or too late to start living well, to achieve our dreams, to realize our goals for happy, fulfilling lives. There's power to be found for our bodies and the vitality inside us all.

And the great news is that part of the solution is right in your own pantry: Quaker Oats. Oats help to build a foundation for a balanced lifestyle, thanks to their whole grain benefits.

NATURALLY GOOD FOR YOU

Throughout the years, from our beginnings in the 1800s, we've used our expertise and pursued unique milling methods that provide wholesome goodness with greater convenience.

The Quaker oat was inspired by the ideals of honesty, purity, and integrity—and the amazing nutritional value of the super grain known as the oat. That's why our original principles hold true today, as our company grows, mills, and prepares Canadian oats to ensure we provide nutritious and tasty oats while we work to lessen our impact on the environment.

Quaker Oats can help you get started on the path to achievement with whole grain goodness that can help with your busy day. Your daily oats can provide you with a key part of the nutrition and energy you need to live the life you're striving for.

ENJOY QUAKER OATS THROUGHOUT THE DAY

That's where this cookbook comes in. It continues our long tradition of sharing recipes, ever since we started putting them on our packages in 1891. We created and selected these recipes to appeal to Canadian appetites, so we know you'll enjoy them. And most important, the recipes are easy to make, and the results taste great!

Just turn the pages to find the perfect dish to help meet your energy needs throughout the day, whether you're sitting down for a meal, entertaining family and friends, or just craving a snack.

Feel the power of Quaker Oats for yourself—and begin to get the most out of life. Quaker. Love Life.

Bon Appétit!

For more recipes and information on the goodness of Quaker Oats, go to www.quakeroats.ca.

WARM UP TO BREAKFAST

MAPLE WALNUT OATMEAL

2   cups/500 mL fat-free (skim) milk

2   tablespoons/30 mL **Aunt Jemima® Original Syrup**

⅛   teaspoon/0.625 mL salt (optional)

⅛   teaspoon/0.625 mL maple extract (optional)

1   cup/250 mL **Quaker® 100% Whole Grain Large Flake Oats** or **Quaker® 100% Whole Grain Quick Oats** (uncooked)

1½ tablespoons/22.5 mL chopped walnuts, toasted

Additional **Aunt Jemima® Original Syrup**

Bring milk, syrup and, if desired, salt and maple extract to a gentle boil in medium saucepan (watch carefully); stir in oats. Return to a boil; reduce heat to medium. Cook 1 minute for quick oats, 5 minutes for large flake oats, or until most of liquid is absorbed, stirring occasionally. Let stand until desired consistency.

Spoon oatmeal into two cereal bowls. Top with walnuts and additional syrup, as desired.

MAKES 2 SERVINGS

HEARTY
BANANA OAT
FLAPJACKS

2 large ripe bananas, peeled and sliced

1 tablespoon/15 mL granulated sugar

1 cup/250 mL all-purpose flour

½ cup/125 mL **Quaker® 100% Whole Grain Large Flake Oats** or **Quaker® 100% Whole Grain Quick Oats** (uncooked)

1 tablespoon/15 mL baking powder

¼ teaspoon/1.25 mL ground cinnamon

¼ teaspoon/1.25 mL salt (optional)

1 cup/250 mL fat-free (skim) milk

1 egg, lightly beaten

2 tablespoons/30 mL vegetable oil

Aunt Jemima® Original Syrup, warmed

Additional banana slices (optional)

Coarsely chopped pecans or walnuts (optional)

Combine banana slices and sugar in medium bowl; stir to coat slices with sugar. Set aside.

Combine flour, oats, baking powder, cinnamon and, if desired, salt in large bowl; mix well. Combine milk, egg and oil in medium bowl; blend well. Add to dry ingredients all at once; stir just until dry ingredients are moistened. (Do not overmix.)

Heat griddle over medium-high heat (or preheat electric skillet or griddle to 375°F/190°C). Lightly grease griddle. For each pancake, pour scant ¼ cup/60 mL batter onto hot griddle. Top with four or five sugar-coated banana slices. Turn pancakes when tops are covered with bubbles and edges look cooked.

Serve with warm syrup and additional banana slices and nuts, if desired.

MAKES 12 PANCAKES

PEACH COBBLER OATMEAL

TOPPING

- ¼ cup/60 mL **Quaker® Kretschmer® Original Toasted Wheat Germ**
- 2 tablespoons/30 mL firmly packed brown sugar
- ¼ teaspoon/1.25 mL ground cinnamon

OATMEAL

- 3 cups/750 mL fat-free (skim) milk
- 1 to 1½ teaspoons/5 to 7.5 mL ground cinnamon
- ½ teaspoon/2.5 mL salt
- ⅛ to ¼ teaspoon/0.625 to 1.25 mL ground nutmeg
- 2 cups/500 mL **Quaker® 100% Whole Grain Large Flake Oats** or **Quaker® 100% Whole Grain Quick Oats** (uncooked)
- 1¼ cups/300 mL chopped frozen (thawed) or canned (drained) peaches
- 1 container (8 ounces/225 grams) low fat or fat-free vanilla yogurt

For topping, combine wheat germ, brown sugar and ¼ teaspoon/1.25 mL cinnamon in small bowl. Set aside.

For oatmeal, bring milk, 1 teaspoon/5 mL cinnamon, salt and nutmeg to a gentle boil in medium saucepan (watch carefully); stir in oats. Return to a boil; reduce heat to medium. Cook 1 minute for quick oats, 5 minutes for large flake oats, stirring occasionally. Stir in peaches. Continue cooking, stirring occasionally, until peaches are heated through and most of liquid is absorbed, about 1 minute.

Spoon oatmeal into four cereal bowls. Top with wheat germ mixture and yogurt.

MAKES 4 SERVINGS

APPLE STREUSEL BAKED OAT PANCAKE

STREUSEL

- ½ cup/125 mL **Quaker® 100% Whole Grain Large Flake Oats** or **Quaker® 100% Whole Grain Quick Oats** (uncooked)
- ¼ cup/60 mL all-purpose flour
- ¼ cup/60 mL firmly packed brown sugar
- 3 tablespoons/45 mL stick margarine or butter, melted

PANCAKE

- ¼ cup/60 mL (½ stick) margarine or butter, cut into pieces
- ⅓ cup/75 mL granulated sugar
- 1 teaspoon/5 mL ground cinnamon
- 3 medium tart apples (about 1¼ pounds/565 grams), cored and cut into thin wedges
- 1 cup/250 mL all-purpose flour
- ½ cup/125 mL **Quaker® 100% Whole Grain Large Flake Oats** or **Quaker® 100% Whole Grain Quick Oats** (uncooked)
- 1 teaspoon/5 mL baking powder
- ¼ teaspoon/1.25 mL salt (optional)
- 1 cup/250 mL fat-free (skim) milk
- 1 egg, lightly beaten

Heat oven to 350°F/180°C.

For streusel, combine ½ cup/125 mL oats, ¼ cup/60 mL flour, brown sugar and melted margarine in small bowl; stir until crumbly. Set aside.

For pancake, place ¼ cup/60 mL margarine into 8-inch square glass baking dish. Place in oven 3 to 5 minutes or until margarine is melted. Remove from oven. Stir in granulated sugar and cinnamon. Add apples; stir until apples are well coated with sugar mixture. Bake 10 to 15 minutes or until apples have softened, stirring occasionally.

Combine 1 cup/250 mL flour, ½ cup/125 mL oats, baking powder and, if desired, salt in large bowl; mix well. Combine milk and egg in small bowl; blend well. Add to dry ingredients all at once; stir just until dry ingredients are moistened. (Do not overmix.) Spoon over apple mixture in baking dish, spreading batter to edges of dish. Sprinkle reserved streusel evenly over batter.

Bake 25 to 30 minutes or until wooden pick inserted in centre comes out with a few moist crumbs clinging to it. Serve immediately.

MAKES 8 SERVINGS

CARAMEL-NUT
STICKY
BISCUITS

TOPPING

- ⅔ cup/150 mL firmly packed brown sugar
- ¼ cup/60 mL light corn syrup
- ¼ cup/60 mL (½ stick) margarine, melted
- ½ teaspoon/2.5 mL ground cinnamon
- 1 cup/250 mL pecan halves

BISCUITS

- 2 cups/500 mL all-purpose flour
- 1 cup/250 mL **Quaker® 100% Whole Grain Large Flake Oats** or **Quaker® 100% Whole Grain Quick Oats** (uncooked)
- ¼ cup/60 mL granulated sugar
- 1 tablespoon/15 mL baking powder
- ¾ teaspoon/3.75 mL baking soda
- ½ teaspoon/2.5 mL ground cinnamon
- ½ teaspoon/2.5 mL salt (optional)
- ⅓ cup/75 mL (⅔ stick) margarine
- 1 cup/250 mL buttermilk

Heat oven to 425°F/220°C.

For topping, combine brown sugar, corn syrup, melted margarine and ½ teaspoon/2.5 mL cinnamon; mix well. Spread onto bottom of 9-inch square baking pan. Sprinkle with pecans. Set aside.

For biscuits, combine flour, oats, granulated sugar, baking powder, baking soda, ½ teaspoon/2.5 mL cinnamon and, if desired, salt in large bowl; mix well. Cut in ⅓ cup/75 mL margarine with pastry blender or two knives until crumbly. Stir in buttermilk, mixing just until moistened. Knead gently on lightly floured surface 5 to 7 times; pat into 8-inch square. Cut with knife into sixteen 2-inch square biscuits; place over topping in pan.

Bake 25 to 28 minutes or until golden brown. Let stand 3 minutes; invert onto large platter. Serve warm.

MAKES 16 SERVINGS

tip

If buttermilk is unavailable, substitute soured milk. Combine 1 tablespoon/15 mL vinegar or lemon juice with enough milk to equal 1 cup/250 mL. Stir well. Let stand 5 minutes before using.

BANANA
BREAD
OATMEAL

3 cups/750 mL fat-free (skim) milk

3 tablespoons/45 mL firmly packed brown sugar

¾ teaspoon/3.75 mL ground cinnamon

¼ teaspoon/1.25 mL ground nutmeg

2 cups/500 mL **Quaker® 100% Whole Grain Large Flake Oats** or **Quaker® 100% Whole Grain Quick Oats** (uncooked)

2 medium-size ripe bananas, mashed (about 1 cup/250 mL)

2 tablespoons/30 mL coarsely chopped toasted pecans

Fat-free vanilla yogurt (optional)

Banana slices (optional)

Pecan halves (optional)

Bring milk, brown sugar, cinnamon and nutmeg to a gentle boil in medium saucepan (watch carefully); stir in oats. Return to a boil; reduce heat to medium. Cook 1 minute for quick oats, 5 minutes for large flake oats, or until most of liquid is absorbed, stirring occasionally.

Remove oatmeal from heat. Stir in mashed bananas and chopped pecans. Spoon oatmeal into six cereal bowls. Top with yogurt, sliced bananas and pecan halves, if desired.

MAKES 6 SERVINGS

tip

To toast pecans, spread evenly in shallow baking pan. Bake at 350°F/180°C 5 to 7 minutes or until light golden brown. Or spread nuts evenly on microwave-safe plate. Microwave on HIGH 1 minute; stir. Continue to microwave on HIGH, checking every 30 seconds until nuts are fragrant and brown.

OATY
PEAR 'N' PECAN
PANCAKES

1 cup/250 mL **Aunt Jemima® Original Pancake Mix**

1 teaspoon/5 mL ground cinnamon

1 cup/250 mL milk

1 egg

1 tablespoon/15 mL vegetable oil

1 medium-firm ripe pear, cored and chopped (about 1 cup/250 mL)

¾ cup/175 mL **Quaker® 100% Whole Grain Large Flake Oats** or **Quaker® 100% Whole Grain Quick Oats** (uncooked)

2 tablespoons/30 mL chopped toasted pecans

½ to ¾ cup/125 to 175 mL **Aunt Jemima® Lite Syrup**, warmed

Pear slices (optional)

Chopped toasted pecans (optional)

Combine pancake mix and cinnamon in large bowl; mix well. Combine milk, egg and oil in medium bowl; mix well. Add to pancake mix; stir with wire whisk just until combined. Gently stir in pear, oats and 2 tablespoons/30 mL pecans. Let stand 1 to 2 minutes to thicken.

Heat griddle over medium-high heat (or preheat electric skillet or griddle to 375°F/190°C). Lightly grease griddle. Cook pancakes on hot griddle according to package directions. Serve with syrup and, if desired, pear slices and additional pecans.

MAKES 12 PANCAKES

tip

To toast pecans, spread evenly in shallow baking pan. Bake at 350°F/180°C 5 to 7 minutes or until light golden brown. Or spread nuts evenly on microwave-safe plate. Microwave on HIGH 1 minute; stir. Continue to microwave on HIGH, checking every 30 seconds until nuts are fragrant and brown..

ORANGE CRANBERRY OATMEAL

2 cups/500 mL **Tropicana Pure Premium**® orange juice

1 cup/250 mL water

¼ teaspoon/1.25 mL salt

⅛ teaspoon/0.625 mL ground cinnamon

2 cups/500 mL **Quaker® 100% Whole Grain Large Flake Oats or Quaker® 100% Whole Grain Quick Oats** (uncooked)

½ cup/125 mL dried cranberries

1 cup/250 mL low fat or fat-free vanilla yogurt

¼ cup/60 mL chopped toasted walnuts

Additional dried cranberries (optional)

Bring orange juice, water, salt and cinnamon to a gentle boil in medium saucepan (watch carefully). Stir in oats and cranberries. Return to a boil; reduce heat to medium. Cook 1 minute for quick oats, 5 minutes for large flake oats, or until most of liquid is absorbed, stirring occasionally. Let stand until desired consistency.

Spoon oatmeal into four cereal bowls. Top each serving with ¼ cup/60 mL yogurt, 1 tablespoon/15 mL walnuts and additional cranberries, if desired.

MAKES 4 SERVINGS

MICROWAVE DIRECTIONS: Combine all ingredients except yogurt and nuts in 3-quart/3-litre microwave-safe bowl. Microwave on HIGH 4 to 6 minutes for quick oats, 7 to 9 minutes for large flake oats, or until most of liquid is absorbed. Let stand until desired consistency. Top each serving with yogurt, walnuts and additional cranberries, if desired.

tip

To toast nuts, spread in single layer on cookie sheet. Bake at 350°F/180°C about 6 to 8 minutes or until lightly browned and fragrant, stirring occasionally. Cool before using. Or spread in single layer on microwave-safe plate. Microwave on HIGH 1 minute; stir. Continue to microwave on HIGH, checking every 30 seconds, until nuts are fragrant and brown. Cool before using.

CREAMY
MAPLE CRANBERRY
OATMEAL

3½ cups/875 mL fat-free (skim) or low fat (2%) milk

2 cups/500 mL **Quaker® 100% Whole Grain Large Flake Oats** or **Quaker® 100% Whole Grain Quick Oats** (uncooked)

½ cup/125 mL dried cranberries

⅓ cup/75 mL **Aunt Jemima® Syrup**, regular or light

¼ cup/60 mL **Quaker® Kretschmer® Original Toasted Wheat Germ**

Additional **Aunt Jemima® Syrup**, milk or yogurt (optional)

tip

Freeze single servings of cooked oatmeal in small resealable freezer bags. Thaw in refrigerator overnight. Transfer to microwave-safe bowl. Microwave, covered, on DEFROST until hot, stirring once or twice.

Bring milk to a gentle boil in medium saucepan (watch carefully). Stir in oats, cranberries and ⅓ cup/75 mL syrup. Return to a boil; reduce heat to medium. Cook 1 minute for quick oats, 5 minutes for large flake oats, or until most of milk is absorbed, stirring occasionally. Let stand until desired consistency. Stir in wheat germ.

Spoon oatmeal into four cereal bowls. Drizzle with additional syrup, if desired. Serve with milk or yogurt, if desired.

MAKES 4 SERVINGS

MICROWAVE DIRECTIONS: Combine all ingredients except wheat germ in 3-quart/3-litre microwave-safe bowl. Microwave on HIGH 6 to 7 minutes for quick oats, 9 to 10 minutes for large flake oats, or until most of liquid is absorbed. Let stand until desired consistency. Stir in wheat germ.

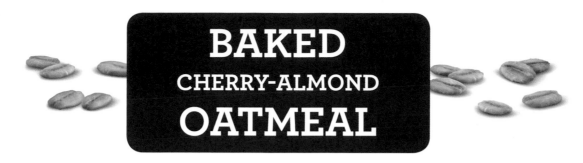

BAKED
CHERRY-ALMOND
OATMEAL

2¼ cups/550 mL **Quaker® 100% Whole Grain Large Flake Oats** or **Quaker® 100% Whole Grain Quick Oats** (uncooked)

½ cup/125 mL firmly packed brown sugar

½ teaspoon/2.5 mL salt

3 cups/750 mL low fat (2%) milk

3 eggs, lightly beaten

1 tablespoon/15 mL melted butter (optional)

1 teaspoon/5 mL vanilla extract

¼ to ½ teaspoon/1.25 to 2.5 mL almond extract

¾ cup/175 mL dried cherries

½ cup/125 mL toasted sliced almonds

Low-fat vanilla yogurt

Heat oven to 350°F/180°C. Spray eight 6-ounce/170-gram custard cups or ramekins with nonstick cooking spray; arrange on rimmed baking sheet.

Combine oats, brown sugar and salt in large bowl; mix well. Whisk together milk, eggs, butter, if desired, vanilla extract and almond extract in medium bowl. Add to dry ingredients; mix until well blended. Spoon into cups. Stir cherries into each cup, dividing evenly; sprinkle evenly with almonds.

Bake until knife inserted near centre comes out clean, about 23 to 26 minutes for quick oats, 25 to 30 minutes for large flake oats. (Centres will not be completely set.) Cool 10 minutes. To serve, top with yogurt.

MAKES 8 SERVINGS

VARIATIONS:

• Substitute dried cranberries, blueberries or chopped dried apricots for dried cherries.

• To bake in 8-inch square baking pan, spray pan with nonstick cooking spray. Prepare oatmeal as directed. Pour into prepared pan, stir in cherries and sprinkle with almonds. Bake until knife inserted near centre comes out clean, about 30 to 35 minutes.

tip

To toast nuts, spread in single layer on cookie sheet. Bake at 350°F/ 180°C about 6 to 8 minutes or until lightly browned and fragrant, stirring occasionally. Cool before using. Or spread in single layer on microwave-safe plate. Microwave on HIGH 1 minute; stir. Continue to microwave on HIGH, checking every 30 seconds, until nuts are fragrant and brown. Cool before using.

PINEAPPLE-
MACADAMIA
OATMEAL

1 can (20 ounces/567 grams) pineapple tidbits in pineapple juice

Water

¼ teaspoon/1.25 mL salt

2 cups/500 mL **Quaker® 100% Whole Grain Large Flake Oats** or **Quaker® 100% Whole Grain Quick Oats** (uncooked)

2 containers (6 ounces/170 grams each) fat-free vanilla yogurt*

¼ to ½ teaspoon/1.25 to 2.5 mL ground ginger

⅓ cup/75 mL firmly packed brown sugar*

¼ cup/60 mL coarsely chopped macadamia nuts or almonds

*If artificially sweetened yogurt is used, reduce brown sugar to ¼ cup/60 mL.

Drain pineapple tidbits, reserving juice. Set fruit aside. Add enough water to juice to equal 3¼ cups/810 mL. Bring combined juice and water and salt to a boil in medium saucepan; stir in oats. Return to a boil; reduce heat to medium. Cook 1 minute for quick oats, 5 minutes for large flake oats, or until most of liquid is absorbed, stirring occasionally. Stir in reserved pineapple. Let stand, covered, until desired consistency.

Spoon yogurt into small bowl. Add ginger; mix well. Spoon oatmeal into five cereal bowls. Top each serving with brown sugar, nuts and yogurt, dividing evenly.

MAKES 5 SERVINGS

BAKED OATMEAL

2 cups/500 mL **Quaker® 100% Whole Grain Quick Oats** or 2¼/550 mL cups **Quaker® 100% Whole Grain Large Flake Oats** (uncooked)

⅓ cup/75 mL granulated sugar

3⅓ cups/825 mL fat-free (skim) milk

2 eggs, lightly beaten or ½ cup/125 mL liquid egg substitute

2 teaspoons/10 mL vanilla extract

⅓ cup/75 mL firmly packed brown sugar

Heat oven to 350°F/180°C. Spray 8-inch square glass baking dish with nonstick cooking spray.

Combine oats and granulated sugar in large bowl. Combine milk, eggs and vanilla extract in medium bowl; mix well. Add to oat mixture; mix well. Pour into baking dish.

Bake 40 to 45 minutes or until centre jiggles slightly. Remove from oven to wire rack.

Sprinkle brown sugar evenly over top of oatmeal. Using back of spoon, gently spread into thin layer across entire surface of oatmeal. Return to oven; bake just until sugar melts, about 2 to 3 minutes. Set oven to broil. Broil 3 inches from heat until sugar bubbles and browns slightly, 1 to 2 minutes. (Watch carefully to prevent burning. It may be necessary to turn baking dish.) Spoon into bowls to serve.

MAKES 8 SERVINGS

PUMPKIN
PECAN
OATMEAL

3   cups/750 mL water

1   teaspoon/5 mL pumpkin pie spice

¼   teaspoon/1.25 mL salt (optional)

2   cups/500 mL **Quaker® 100% Whole Grain Large Flake Oats** or **Quaker® 100% Whole Grain Quick Oats** (uncooked)

1   cup/250 mL canned pumpkin

⅓   cup/75 mL firmly packed brown sugar

1   container (8 ounces/225 grams) low fat or fat-free vanilla yogurt

3   tablespoons/45 mL coarsely chopped toasted pecans

To toast pecans, spread evenly in shallow baking pan. Bake at 400°F/200°C 5 to 7 minutes or until deep golden brown. Or, spread nuts evenly on microwave-safe plate. Microwave on HIGH 1 minute; stir. Continue to microwave on HIGH, checking every 30 seconds until nuts are fragrant and brown.

To make your own pumpkin pie spice, combine 4 teaspoons/ 20 mL ground cinnamon, 1 teaspoon/5 mL ground ginger, ½ teaspoon/2.5 mL ground allspice, ½ teaspoon/2.5 mL ground cloves and ½ teaspoon/2.5 mL ground nutmeg in a small container with a tight-fitting lid. Store in cool, dark cabinet.

Bring water, pumpkin pie spice and, if desired, salt to a boil in medium saucepan; stir in oats. Return to a boil; reduce heat to medium. Cook 1 minute for quick oats, 5 minutes for large flake oats, or until most of liquid is absorbed, stirring occasionally. Stir in pumpkin and brown sugar; cook 1 minute. Let stand until desired consistency.

Spoon oatmeal into four cereal bowls. Top with yogurt and pecans.

MAKES 4 SERVINGS

MICROWAVE DIRECTIONS: Combine water, pumpkin pie spice, salt and oats in 3-quart/3-litre microwave-safe bowl. Microwave on HIGH 6 to 7 minutes for quick oats, 9 to 10 minutes for large flake oats, or until most of liquid is absorbed. Stir in pumpkin and brown sugar. Microwave on HIGH 30 to 60 seconds. Let stand until desired consistency.

APRICOT
HONEY
OATMEAL

3½ cups/875 mL water

⅓ cup/75 mL chopped dried apricots

¼ cup/60 mL honey

½ teaspoon/2.5 mL ground cinnamon

2 cups/500 mL **Quaker® 100% Whole Grain Large Flake Oats** or **Quaker® 100% Whole Grain Quick Oats** (uncooked)

Bring water, apricots, honey and cinnamon to a boil in 3-quart/3-litre saucepan; stir in oats. Return to a boil; reduce heat to medium. Cook 1 minute for quick oats, 5 minutes for large flake oats, or until most of liquid is absorbed, stirring occasionally. Let stand until desired consistency.

MAKES 4 SERVINGS

tip

If desired, substitute raisins, dried peaches or pears, dried cranberries or blueberries, dried apples, dates or diced mixed dried fruit for the apricots.

CINNAMON ROLL PANCAKES

GLAZE

½ cup/125 mL light cream cheese (from a tub)

½ teaspoon/2.5 mL ground cinnamon

⅓ cup/75 mL **Aunt Jemima® Original Syrup**

PANCAKES

2 cups/500 mL **Aunt Jemima® Complete Buttermilk Pancake & Waffle Mix**

½ cup/125 mL golden or dark raisins (optional)

1¼ teaspoons/6.25 mL ground cinnamon

1½ cups/350 mL water

1⅓ cups/325 mL **Quaker® Life® Toasted Cinnamon Cereal**

½ cup/125 mL **Aunt Jemima® Original Syrup**

For glaze, combine cream cheese and ½ teaspoon/2.5 mL cinnamon in small bowl. Gradually add ⅓ cup/75 mL syrup, stirring with wire whisk until smooth. Set aside.

For pancakes, combine pancake mix, raisins, if desired, and 1¼ teaspoons/ 6.25 mL cinnamon in medium bowl. Add water; stir with wire whisk just until large lumps disappear.

Heat griddle over medium-high heat (or preheat electric skillet or griddle to 375°F/190°C). Lightly grease griddle. For each pancake, pour scant ¼ cup/ 60 mL batter onto hot griddle; sprinkle with heaping 1 tablespoon/15 mL cereal.

Turn when pancakes bubble and bottoms are golden brown. Drizzle with glaze. Serve with syrup.

MAKES 16 PANCAKES

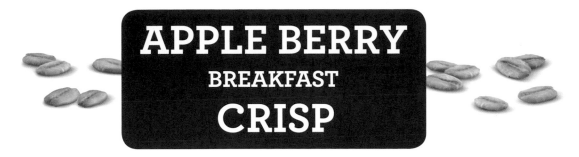

APPLE BERRY
BREAKFAST
CRISP

FILLING

- 4 cups/1 litre thinly sliced peeled apples (about 4 medium)
- 2 cups/500 mL fresh or frozen blueberries or sliced strawberries
- ¼ cup/60 mL firmly packed brown sugar
- ¼ cup/60 mL frozen orange juice concentrate, thawed
- 2 tablespoons/30 mL all-purpose flour
- 1 teaspoon/5 mL ground cinnamon

TOPPING

- 1 cup/250 mL **Quaker® 100% Whole Grain Large Flake Oats** or **Quaker® 100% Whole Grain Quick Oats** (uncooked)
- ½ cup/125 mL firmly packed brown sugar
- ⅓ cup/75 mL (⅔ stick) margarine or butter, melted
- 2 tablespoons/30 mL all-purpose flour

Heat oven to 350°F/180°C. Spray 8-inch square glass baking dish with nonstick cooking spray.

For filling, combine apples, blueberries, brown sugar, juice concentrate, flour and cinnamon in large bowl; stir until fruit is evenly coated. Spoon into baking dish.

For topping, combine oats, brown sugar, margarine and flour in medium bowl; mix until crumbly. Sprinkle evenly over fruit.

Bake 30 to 35 minutes or until apples are tender. Serve warm.

MAKES 9 SERVINGS

tip

For a delicious dessert, serve warm with vanilla frozen yogurt.

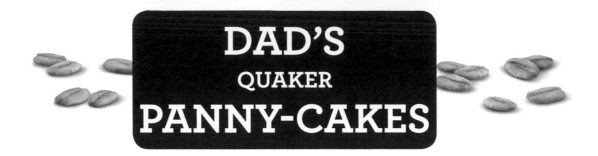

DAD'S
QUAKER
PANNY-CAKES

2 cups/500 mL **Aunt Jemima® Complete** or **Buttermilk Complete Pancake & Waffle Mix**

1 packet **Quaker® Instant Oatmeal**, any flavour (uncooked)

1½ cups/350 mL water

1½ cups/350 mL **Aunt Jemima® Original Syrup**

Combine pancake mix and oatmeal in medium bowl; mix well. Add water; stir with wire whisk until large lumps disappear.

Heat griddle over medium-high heat (or preheat electric skillet or griddle to 375°F/190°C). Lightly grease griddle. Prepare pancakes according to package directions. Serve warm with syrup.

MAKES 12 PANCAKES

ORANGE
BANANA DATE
OATMEAL

2 cups/500 mL **Tropicana Pure Premium®** orange juice or **Dole®** 100% orange juice

1 cup/250 mL water

¼ teaspoon/1.25 mL salt (optional)

⅛ teaspoon/0.625 mL ground nutmeg

1½ cups/350 mL **Quaker® 100% Whole Grain Large Flake Oats** or **Quaker® 100% Whole Grain Quick Oats** (uncooked)

¾ cup/175 mL chopped dates or raisins

1 medium-size ripe banana, mashed

Bring juice, water, salt, if desired, and nutmeg to a gentle boil in medium saucepan; stir in oats and dates. Return to a boil; reduce heat to medium. Cook 1 minute for quick oats, 5 minutes for large flake oats, or until most of liquid is absorbed, stirring occasionally.

Stir in banana. Let stand until desired consistency.

MAKES 4 SERVINGS

BERRY
ALMOND CRUMBLE
OATMEAL

TOPPING

- ½   cup/125 mL **Quaker® 100% Whole Grain Large Flake Oats** or **Quaker® 100% Whole Grain Quick Oats** (uncooked)
- ¼   cup/60 mL sliced almonds
- ⅓   cup/75 mL firmly packed brown sugar
- ½   teaspoon/2.5 mL ground cinnamon

OATMEAL

- 3   cups/750 mL fat-free (skim) milk or low fat soy drink
- 1½ teaspoons/7.5 mL ground cinnamon
- 2   cups/500 mL **Quaker® 100% Whole Grain Large Flake Oats** or **Quaker® 100% Whole Grain Quick Oats** (uncooked)
- 1   cup/250 mL blueberries, frozen (do not thaw) or canned (drained)

For topping, combine oats and almonds in medium skillet. Cook over medium-low heat 4 to 6 minutes, stirring occasionally, until both are lightly browned. Cool completely. Combine brown sugar and ½ teaspoon/2.5 mL cinnamon in small bowl. Add oat mixture; mix well. Set aside.

For oatmeal, bring milk and 1½ teaspoons/7.5 mL cinnamon to a gentle boil in medium saucepan (watch carefully); stir in oats. Return to a boil; reduce heat to medium. Cook 1 minute for quick oats, 5 minutes for large flake oats, stirring occasionally. Gently stir in blueberries. Continue cooking, until blueberries are heated through and most of liquid is absorbed, about 1 minute.

Spoon oatmeal into five cereal bowls. Sprinkle topping over oatmeal.

MAKES 5 SERVINGS

tips

To toast oats and almonds in microwave oven, combine oats and almonds in glass pie plate. Heat on HIGH 2 to 4 minutes or until light golden brown, stirring every minute. Cool completely. Proceed as directed.

To toast oats and almonds in oven, heat oven to 350°F/180°C. Place oats in shallow baking pan. Bake 5 minutes, stirring once. Add almonds and continue baking 5 minutes, stirring occasionally, until oats and almonds are golden brown. Cool completely. Proceed as directed.

COOL BREAKFAST CHOICES

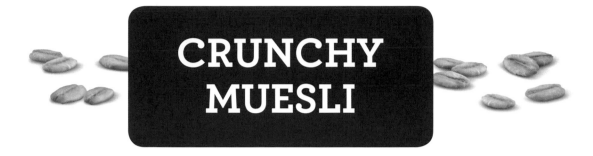

CRUNCHY MUESLI

1½ cups/350 mL fat-free (skim) milk

1¼ cups/300 mL **Quaker® 100% Whole Grain Large Flake Oats** or **Quaker® 100% Whole Grain Quick Oats** (uncooked)

¼ cup/60 mL raisins

¼ cup/60 mL sweetened dried cranberries

¾ cup/175 mL sweetened condensed milk

3 tablespoons/45 mL lemon juice

1 medium Granny Smith apple, unpeeled, cut into thin strips

2 tablespoons/30 mL slivered almonds

1 teaspoon/5 mL nuts and seeds, chopped

Mint leaves (optional)

Combine milk, oats, raisins and cranberries in medium bowl; cover and refrigerate overnight.

Remove oat mixture from refrigerator; drain any excess liquid.

Add condensed milk, lemon juice, apple, almonds and nut/seed mixture; mix well. If desired, garnish with mint.

MAKES 2 TO 3 SERVINGS

SUNSHINE MORNING GRANOLA

2   cups/500 mL **Quaker® 100% Whole Grain Large Flake Oats** or **Quaker® 100% Whole Grain Quick Oats** (uncooked)

⅓   cup/75 mL honey

2   tablespoons/30 mL chopped pecans

2   tablespoons/30 mL vegetable oil

2   teaspoons/10 mL grated orange peel

1   teaspoon/5 mL vanilla extract

¼   teaspoon/1.25 mL ground cinnamon

⅛   teaspoon/0.625 mL salt

⅔   cup/150 mL diced dried mixed fruit (about 3 ounces/90 grams)

Heat oven to 350°F/180°C.

Combine all ingredients except dried fruit in large bowl; mix well. Spread evenly in 15×10-inch jelly-roll pan or 13×9-inch baking pan.

Bake 20 to 25 minutes or until golden brown, stirring once after 10 minutes. Cool completely in pan. Stir in dried fruit. Store tightly covered up to five days.

MAKES 3½ CUPS/875 ML

SERVING SUGGESTIONS:
• Layer with low fat yogurt as a breakfast parfait.
• Serve with milk as a breakfast cereal.
• Stir into low fat yogurt for a quick snack.
• Sprinkle over fresh fruit, ice cream or frozen yogurt for a flavourful dessert.

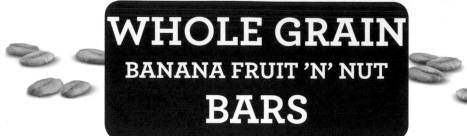

WHOLE GRAIN
BANANA FRUIT 'N' NUT
BARS

1¼ cups/300 mL whole wheat flour

2 teaspoons/10 mL pumpkin pie spice

½ teaspoon/2.5 mL baking soda

¼ teaspoon/1.25 mL salt

⅔ cup/150 mL firmly packed brown sugar

½ cup/125 mL (1 stick) light butter

1¼ cups/300 mL mashed ripe bananas (about 3 small bananas)

1 large egg

1½ cups/350 mL **Quaker® 100% Whole Grain Large Flake Oats** or **Quaker® 100% Whole Grain Quick Oats** (uncooked)

⅔ cup/150 mL chopped pitted dates or golden raisins

⅔ cup/150 mL chopped toasted walnuts

Heat oven to 350°F/180°C. Lightly spray 13×9-inch metal baking pan with nonstick cooking spray. Stir together flour, pumpkin pie spice, baking soda and salt in medium bowl; mix well. Set aside.

Beat brown sugar and butter in large bowl with electric mixer until well blended. Add bananas and egg; mix well. (Mixture will look curdled.) Add flour mixture; beat at low speed just until well blended. Stir in oats, dates and walnuts. Spread evenly in prepared pan.

Bake 20 to 25 minutes, until edges are golden brown and wooden pick inserted in centre comes out with a few moist crumbs clinging to it. Cool completely in pan on wire rack. Cut into bars.

MAKES 24 BARS

tips

To store, wrap tightly in foil and store up to two days at room temperature. For longer storage, label and freeze in airtight container up to three months. Defrost, uncovered, at room temperature.

To toast nuts, spread in single layer on cookie sheet. Bake at 350°F/180°C 6 to 8 minutes or until lightly browned and fragrant, stirring occasionally. Cool before using. Or spread in single layer on microwave-safe plate. Microwave on HIGH 1 minute; stir. Continue to microwave on HIGH, checking every 30 seconds, until nuts are fragrant and brown. Cool before using.

FRUITFUL
MORNING
MUESLI

2   cups/500 mL **Quaker® 100% Whole Grain Large Flake Oats** or **Quaker® 100% Whole Grain Quick Oats** (uncooked)

2   cups/500 mL apple juice or apricot nectar

1½ cups/350 mL sliced fresh fruit (any combination of banana, peaches, nectarines or strawberries)

1   container (8 ounces/225 grams) low fat vanilla yogurt

2   tablespoons/30 mL chopped nuts (optional)

Combine all ingredients except nuts; mix well.

Cover; refrigerate 8 hours or overnight.

Serve cold; sprinkle with nuts, if desired. Refrigerate in airtight container up to four days.

MAKES 4 SERVINGS

tip

For extra flavour, toast nuts by spreading them evenly in small shallow baking pan. Bake at 350°F/180°C 5 to 8 minutes or until light golden brown, stirring occasionally. Or, spread nuts on microwave-safe plate. Microwave on HIGH 1 minute; stir. Continue microwaving, checking every 30 seconds, until nuts are crunchy.

FRUIT
AND HONEY
GRANOLA

3½ cups/875 mL **Quaker® 100% Whole Grain Large Flake Oats** or **Quaker® 100% Whole Grain Quick Oats** (uncooked)

2 tablespoons/30 mL coarsely chopped pecans

½ cup/125 mL honey

2 tablespoons/30 mL vegetable oil

1 teaspoon/5 mL vanilla extract

½ teaspoon/2.5 mL ground cinnamon

⅛ to ¼ teaspoon/0.625 to 1.25 mL salt (optional)

1 package (6 ounces/170 grams) diced dried mixed fruit (about 1⅓ cups/325 mL)

Heat oven to 350°F/180°C.

Combine oats and pecans in large bowl; mix well. Spread evenly in 15×10-inch jelly-roll pan or on rimmed baking sheet. Combine honey, oil, vanilla extract, cinnamon and, if desired, salt in small bowl; mix well. Pour over oat mixture; mix well.

Bake 30 to 35 minutes or until golden brown, stirring every 10 minutes. Cool completely in pan. Stir in dried fruit. Store tightly covered up to one week.

MAKES 11 SERVINGS

VARIATION: Substitute dried cranberries, chopped dried apricots or chopped dried peaches for dried mixed fruit.

BERRY POWER DRINK

1 cup/250 mL fruit juice (such as orange, cranberry or apple)

1 cup/250 mL fresh or frozen strawberries

1 container (8 ounces/ 225 grams) low fat vanilla yogurt

⅔ cup/150 mL **Quaker® 100% Whole Grain Large Flake Oats or Quaker® 100% Whole Grain Quick Oats** (uncooked)

1 cup/250 mL ice cubes

Granulated sugar, to taste

Place juice, strawberries, yogurt and oats in blender container. Cover; blend on high speed about 2 minutes or until smooth.

Add ice gradually; blend on high speed an additional minute or until smooth. Blend in sugar to taste.

Serve immediately.

MAKES 2 SERVINGS

CHRISTMAS GRANOLA

4   cups/1 litre **Quaker® 100% Whole Grain Large Flake Oats** or **Quaker® 100% Whole Grain Quick Oats** (uncooked)

½   cup/125 mL shredded coconut

½   cup/125 mL chopped pecans

½   cup/125 mL honey

¼   cup/60 mL raw unsalted sunflower seeds (optional)

¼   cup/60 mL (½ stick) butter or margarine, melted

2   teaspoons/10 mL grated orange peel

1   teaspoon/5 mL vanilla extract

½   teaspoon/2.5 mL ground cinnamon

¼   teaspoon/1.25 mL salt (optional)

1   package (6 ounces/170 grams) dried cranberries (about 1⅓ cups/325 mL)

Heat oven to 350°F/180°C.

Combine all ingredients except cranberries in large bowl; mix well. Spread evenly in 15×10-inch jelly-roll pan.

Bake 40 minutes or until golden brown, stirring every 10 minutes. Cool completely in pan. Stir in cranberries. Store tightly covered up to two weeks.

MAKES 6½ CUPS/1625 ML

VARIATION: For gift giving, spoon granola into airtight glass or plastic jars, canisters, cellophane gift bags (tie closed with ribbon), or empty oatmeal tubes. Ahead of time, paint designs on jars with paint markers or sponges and paint, decorate gift bags with holiday stickers, or cover oatmeal tubes with gift wrap.

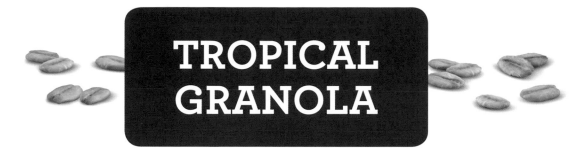

TROPICAL GRANOLA

3½ cups/875 mL **Quaker® 100% Whole Grain Large Flake Oats or Quaker® 100% Whole Grain Quick Oats** (uncooked)

⅓ cup/75 mL coarsely chopped slivered almonds

2 tablespoons/30 mL finely chopped crystallized ginger (optional)

½ cup/125 mL honey

¼ cup/60 mL (½ stick) butter or margarine, melted

1½ to 2 teaspoons/7.5 to 10 mL ground ginger

¼ teaspoon/1.25 mL salt

¾ cup/175 mL chopped dried tropical fruit mix

Heat oven to 350°F/180°C.

Combine oats, almonds and, if desired, crystallized ginger in large bowl; mix well. Combine honey, butter, ground ginger and salt in small bowl; blend well. Drizzle over oat mixture; mix well. Spread evenly in 15×10-inch jelly-roll pan.

Bake 18 to 20 minutes, stirring every 5 minutes. Cool completely in pan. Stir in dried fruit. Store tightly covered up to one week.

MAKES 4½ CUPS/1125 ML

SERVING SUGGESTIONS:
- Layer with low fat yogurt as a breakfast parfait.
- Serve with milk as a breakfast cereal.
- Stir into low fat yogurt for a quick snack.
- Sprinkle over fresh fruit, ice cream or frozen yogurt for a flavourful dessert.

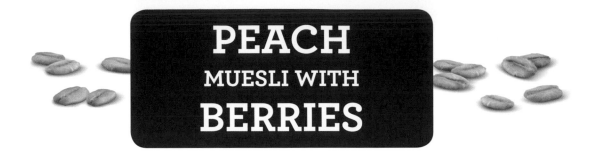

PEACH
MUESLI WITH
BERRIES

2 cups/500 mL **Quaker® 100% Whole Grain Large Flake Oats** or **Quaker® 100% Whole Grain Quick Oats** (uncooked)

2 cups/500 mL coarsely chopped fresh (peeled) or frozen (thawed) peaches

1½ cups/350 mL apple juice

1 container (8 ounces/225 grams) fat-free vanilla or peach yogurt

½ teaspoon/2.5 mL vanilla extract

1 cup/250 mL fresh or frozen (thawed) raspberries or blueberries

To peel fresh peaches easily, place peaches in boiling water 1 minute. Drain; rinse under cold water to cool. Remove peel with a knife.

Combine all ingredients except berries in large bowl; mix well. Cover and refrigerate 8 hours or overnight.

Serve muesli cold topped with berries. Store covered in refrigerator up to four days.

MAKES 4 SERVINGS

GINGERSNAP GRANOLA

4 cups/1 litre **Quaker® Oatmeal Squares™ Cereal**

2 cups/500 mL **Quaker® 100% Whole Grain Large Flake Oats** or **Quaker® 100% Whole Grain Quick Oats** (uncooked)

2 tablespoons/30 mL margarine (vegetable oil spread in sticks)

½ cup/125 mL honey

2 tablespoons/30 mL molasses

2 teaspoons/10 mL grated lemon peel

1 teaspoon/5 mL vanilla extract

½ teaspoon/2.5 mL ground ginger

½ teaspoon/2.5 mL ground cinnamon

Heat oven to 350°F/180°C. Spray 15×10-inch jelly-roll pan with nonstick cooking spray.

Combine cereal and oats in large bowl. Set aside.

Microwave margarine in 2-cup/500-mL microwave-safe bowl on HIGH 30 seconds or until melted. Stir in honey, molasses, lemon peel, vanilla extract, ginger and cinnamon; mix well. Drizzle over cereal mixture; stir to coat evenly. Spread mixture onto baking sheet.

Bake 15 to 18 minutes or until lightly browned, stirring after 10 minutes. Cool completely in pan. Store tightly covered up to two weeks.

MAKES ABOUT 6 CUPS/1.5 LITRES

MICHAEL ROMANO'S
COOL & CREAMY
OATMEAL

1   medium apple, peeled and grated (about ⅔ cup/150 mL) or ¼ cup/60 mL applesauce

½   cup/125 mL **Quaker® 100% Whole Grain Large Flake Oats** or **Quaker® 100% Whole Grain Quick Oats** (uncooked)

½   cup/125 mL fat-free plain, vanilla or fruit-flavoured yogurt

½   cup/125 mL apple juice, apple cider, fat-free (skim) milk or milk substitute

1   tablespoon/15 mL whole almonds, coarsely chopped

1   tablespoon/15 mL raisins or chopped dates

1   teaspoon/5 mL sunflower or pumpkin seeds

    Pinch of ground cinnamon

Combine all ingredients in medium storage container; mix well. Cover; refrigerate overnight. Serve cold.

MAKES 1 SERVING

GOOD
FOR YOU
GRANOLA

3½ cups/875 mL **Quaker® 100% Whole Grain Large Flake Oats** or
Quaker® 100% Whole Grain Quick Oats (uncooked)

¼ cup/60 mL sliced unblanched almonds

¼ cup/60 mL chopped walnuts

⅓ cup/75 mL honey

¼ cup/60 mL vegetable oil

1 teaspoon/5 mL ground cinnamon

1 teaspoon/5 mL vanilla extract

¼ teaspoon/1.25 mL ground nutmeg

Heat oven to 350°F/180°C.

Combine oats, almonds and walnuts in large bowl. Stir together honey, oil, cinnamon, vanilla extract and nutmeg in small bowl. Drizzle over oat mixture; mix well. Spread evenly in 13×9-inch baking pan.

Bake 15 to 20 minutes or until golden brown, stirring every 5 minutes. Remove from oven; cool completely in pan on wire rack. Store tightly covered up to two weeks.

MAKES 4 CUPS/1 LITRE

BREAKFAST AND BRUNCH TREATS

BERRY-LICIOUS
LEMON STREUSEL
CAKE

STREUSEL

1 cup/250 mL **Quaker® 100% Whole Grain Large Flake Oats** or **Quaker® 100% Whole Grain Quick Oats** (uncooked)

¼ cup/60 mL firmly packed brown sugar

¼ cup/60 mL all-purpose flour

¼ cup/60 mL (½ stick) margarine or butter, melted

CAKE

1 package (18.5 ounces/525 grams) yellow cake mix

¾ cup/175 mL **Quaker® 100% Whole Grain Large Flake Oats** or **Quaker® 100% Whole Grain Quick Oats** (uncooked)

1 cup/250 mL water

⅓ cup/75 mL low fat plain yogurt

3 egg whites

1 tablespoon/15 mL grated lemon peel

½ cup/125 mL fresh raspberries

½ cup/125 mL fresh or frozen blueberries

Heat oven to 350°F/180°C. Lightly spray and flour sides and bottom of 13×9-inch metal baking pan with nonstick cooking spray.

For streusel, combine all ingredients in small bowl; mix until crumbly. Set aside.

For cake, combine cake mix, ¾ cup/175 mL oats, water, yogurt, egg whites and lemon peel in large bowl; blend at low speed until moistened. Beat at medium speed 2 minutes. Gently fold berries into batter. Pour into prepared pan. Sprinkle streusel evenly over top of batter, patting gently.

Bake 35 to 37 minutes or until wooden pick inserted in centre comes out clean. Cool completely on wire rack.

MAKES 16 SERVINGS

CRANBERRY ORANGE BREAD

½ cup/125 mL all-purpose flour

1½ cups/350 mL whole wheat flour

1¼ cups/300 mL **Quaker® 100% Whole Grain Large Flake Oats** or **Quaker® 100% Whole Grain Quick Oats** (uncooked)

½ cup/125 mL firmly packed brown sugar

1 teaspoon/5 mL baking powder

½ teaspoon/2.5 mL baking soda

¼ teaspoon/1.25 mL salt

¼ teaspoon/1.25 mL ground nutmeg

½ teaspoon/2.5 mL ground cinnamon

1 cup/250 mL fat-free (skim) milk

3 eggs, lightly beaten

⅓ cup/75 mL **Tropicana Pure Premium®** orange juice or **Dole® 100% orange juice**

¼ cup/60 mL vegetable oil

1 tablespoon/15 mL grated orange peel

¾ cup/175 mL chopped fresh, frozen (thawed) or dried cranberries

2 tablespoons/30 mL chopped pecans

tip

To toast nuts for extra flavour, spread evenly in shallow baking pan. Bake at 350°F/180°C 5 to 10 minutes or until golden brown, stirring occasionally. Cool completely before using.

Heat oven to 350°F/180°C. Spray bottom only of 9×5-inch loaf pan with nonstick cooking spray.

Combine all-purpose flour, whole wheat flour, oats, brown sugar, baking powder, baking soda, salt, nutmeg and cinnamon in large bowl; mix well. Combine milk, eggs, orange juice, oil and orange peel in medium bowl; blend well. Add to dry ingredients all at once; stir just until dry ingredients are moistened. (Do not overmix). Stir in cranberries and pecans. Pour batter into prepared pan.

Bake 60 to 70 minutes or until wooden pick inserted in centre comes out clean. Cool 10 minutes in pan on wire rack. Remove from pan. Cool completely. Store tightly wrapped.

MAKES 12 TO 16 SERVINGS

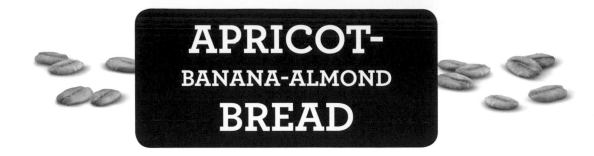

APRICOT-
BANANA-ALMOND
BREAD

2½ cups/600 mL all-purpose flour, plus flour for dusting pan

1 cup/250 mL **Quaker® 100% Whole Grain Large Flake Oats** or **Quaker® 100% Whole Grain Quick Oats** (uncooked)

2 teaspoons/10 mL baking powder

1 teaspoon/5 mL baking soda

½ teaspoon/2.5 mL salt

⅔ cup/150 mL finely chopped dried apricots

¼ cup plus 2 tablespoons/90 mL unblanched sliced almonds, divided

1 cup/250 mL mashed ripe bananas (about 2 medium bananas)

½ cup/125 mL low fat buttermilk

⅓ cup/75 mL vegetable oil

⅓ cup/75 mL firmly packed light brown sugar

2 eggs

¼ teaspoon/1.25 mL almond extract

If buttermilk is unavailable, substitute soured milk. Combine 1 tablespoon/15 mL vinegar or lemon juice with enough milk to equal 1 cup/250 mL. Stir well. Let stand 5 minutes before using.

To store, wrap covered bread tightly in aluminum foil and store up to three days at room temperature. For longer storage, label and freeze.

Heat oven to 350°F/180°C. Spray bottom only of 9×5-inch loaf pan with nonstick cooking spray. Coat bottom of pan with flour; tap out excess.

Combine flour, oats, baking powder, baking soda and salt in large bowl; mix well. Add apricots and ¼ cup/60 mL almonds; mix well.

Whisk together bananas, buttermilk, oil, brown sugar, eggs and almond extract in medium bowl until well blended. Add to dry ingredients all at once; stir just until dry ingredients are evenly moistened. (Do not overmix.) Pour into prepared pan. Sprinkle with remaining 2 tablespoons/30 mL almonds.

Bake 55 to 65 minutes or until golden brown and wooden pick inserted in centre comes out clean. Cool 10 minutes in pan on wire rack. Remove bread from pan. Cool completely on rack.

MAKES 12 TO 16 SERVINGS

OATMEAL
CARROT CAKE
BREAD

1 cup/250 mL **Quaker® 100% Whole Grain Large Flake Oats** or **Quaker® 100% Whole Grain Quick Oats** (uncooked)

½ cup/125 mL fat-free (skim) milk

1 can (8 ounces/225 grams) crushed pineapple in juice, undrained

2 large eggs, lightly beaten

¼ cup/60 mL vegetable oil

1 teaspoon/5 mL vanilla extract

1½ cups/350 mL all-purpose flour

1 cup/250 mL whole wheat flour

1 cup/250 mL firmly packed brown sugar

1 tablespoon/15 mL baking powder

½ teaspoon/2.5 mL baking soda

½ teaspoon/2.5 mL ground cinnamon

¼ teaspoon/1.25 mL salt

1½ cups/350 mL shredded carrots (about 3 medium)

½ cup/125 mL raisins

½ cup/125 mL chopped walnuts

Heat oven to 350°F/180°C. Lightly grease or spray bottom only of two 8×4-inch loaf pans or one 9×5-inch loaf pan with nonstick cooking spray.

Combine oats and milk in medium bowl; mix well. Let stand 10 minutes. Add pineapple (including juice), eggs, oil and vanilla extract; mix well.

Combine all-purpose flour, whole wheat flour, brown sugar, baking powder, baking soda, cinnamon and salt in large bowl; mix well. Stir in carrots, raisins and walnuts. Add oat mixture to dry ingredients all at once; stir just until dry ingredients are moistened. (Do not overmix.) Pour batter into prepared pans.

Bake 45 to 55 minutes for 8×4-inch pans (60 to 75 minutes for 9×5-inch pan) or until wooden pick inserted in centre comes out clean and crust is golden brown. Cool 10 minutes in pan on wire rack. Remove from pan. Cool completely. Store tightly wrapped.

MAKES 12 TO 16 SERVINGS

BEST BANANA BREAD

- 1 cup/250 mL **Quaker® 100% Whole Grain Large Flake Oats** or **Quaker® 100% Whole Grain Quick Oats** (uncooked)
- ½ cup/125 mL fat-free (skim) milk
- 1 cup/250 mL mashed very ripe bananas (about 3 medium)
- ½ cup/125 mL liquid egg substitute or 4 egg whites, lightly beaten
- ½ cup/125 mL vegetable oil
- 2 cups/500 mL all-purpose flour
- 2 tablespoons/30 mL heat-stable sugar substitute equal to ¼ cup/60 mL sugar
- 2 teaspoons/10 mL baking powder
- 1 teaspoon/5 mL ground cinnamon
- ½ teaspoon/2.5 mL baking soda
- ½ teaspoon/2.5 mL salt (optional)
- ½ teaspoon/2.5 mL ground nutmeg

Heat oven to 350°F/180°C. Lightly spray bottom only of 9×5-inch loaf pan with nonstick cooking spray.

Combine oats and milk in medium bowl; mix well. Let stand 10 minutes. Add bananas, egg substitute and oil; mix well.

Combine flour, sweetener, baking powder, cinnamon, baking soda, salt, if desired, and nutmeg in large bowl; mix well. Add oat mixture to dry ingredients all at once; stir just until dry ingredients are moistened. (Do not overmix.) Pour into prepared pan.

Bake 55 to 65 minutes or until wooden pick inserted in centre comes out clean. Cool 10 minutes in pan on wire rack. Remove from pan. Cool completely. Store tightly wrapped.

MAKES 12 TO 16 SERVINGS

BANANA-NANA
PECAN
BREAD

1 cup/250 mL **Quaker® 100% Whole Grain Large Flake Oats or Quaker® 100% Whole Grain Quick Oats** (uncooked)

½ cup/125 mL chopped pecans

3 tablespoons/45 mL margarine or butter, melted

2 tablespoons/30 mL firmly packed brown sugar

1 package (14 ounces/ 398 grams) banana bread quick bread mix

1 cup/250 mL water

½ cup/125 mL mashed ripe banana (about 1 large)

2 eggs, lightly beaten

3 tablespoons/45 mL canola oil

Heat oven to 375°F/190°C. Grease and flour bottom only of 9×5-inch loaf pan.

Combine oats, pecans, margarine and brown sugar in small bowl; mix well. Reserve ½ cup/125 mL mixture. Set aside. Combine remaining oat mixture, quick bread mix, water, banana, eggs and oil in large bowl. Mix just until dry ingredients are moistened. Pour into prepared pan. Sprinkle top of loaf with reserved oat mixture.

Bake 50 to 55 minutes or until wooden pick inserted in centre comes out clean. Cool 10 minutes in pan; remove to wire rack. Cool completely.

MAKES 12 TO 16 SERVINGS

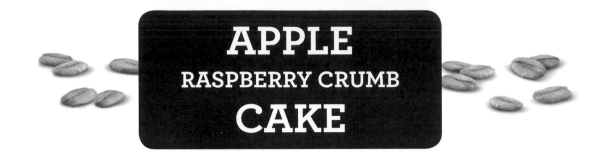

APPLE
RASPBERRY CRUMB
CAKE

CRUMB CAKE

1½ cups/350 mL all-purpose flour

¾ cup/175 mL **Quaker® 100% Whole Grain Large Flake Oats** or **Quaker® 100% Whole Grain Quick Oats** (uncooked)

¾ cup/175 mL granulated sugar

1 teaspoon/5 mL ground cinnamon

½ teaspoon/2.5 mL baking powder

½ teaspoon/2.5 mL baking soda

½ teaspoon/2.5 mL ground nutmeg

¼ teaspoon/1.25 mL salt (optional)

½ cup/125 mL (1 stick) butter, chilled

¼ cup/60 mL part-skim ricotta cheese

¾ cup/175 mL fat-free or reduced-fat sour cream

2 egg whites, lightly beaten

FILLING

2 cups/500 mL chopped peeled apples (about 2 medium)

⅓ cup/75 mL seedless raspberry jam

⅔ teaspoon/3.5 mL all-purpose flour

Powdered sugar

Heat oven to 350°F/180°C. Lightly grease or spray 9-inch springform pan or round metal cake pan with nonstick cooking spray.

For cake and topping, combine 1½ cups/350 mL flour, oats, granulated sugar, cinnamon, baking powder, baking soda, nutmeg and salt, if desired, in large bowl; mix well. Cut in butter and ricotta cheese with pastry blender or two knives until crumbly. Reserve 1½ cups/350 mL oat mixture for topping. Set aside.

Combine sour cream and egg whites in small bowl; add to remaining oat mixture, mixing just until moistened. Spread batter over bottom and ½ inch up sides of pan.

For filling, combine apples, jam and ⅔ teaspoon/3.5 mL flour; spoon over cake. Sprinkle reserved oat mixture over fruit.

Bake 50 to 55 minutes or until golden brown and centre is firm to touch. Sprinkle with powdered sugar. Serve warm.

MAKES 12 TO 16 SERVINGS

QUICK
ALMOND OAT DANISH
COFFEE CAKE

1 cup plus 2 tablespoons/280 mL **Quaker® 100% Whole Grain Large Flake Oats or Quaker® 100% Whole Grain Quick Oats** (uncooked), divided

5 tablespoons/75 mL margarine or butter, melted

⅓ cup/75 mL finely chopped almonds

⅓ cup/75 mL granulated sugar

2 tablespoons/30 mL egg substitute or 1 egg white, lightly beaten, divided

¾ teaspoon/3.75 mL almond extract

1 pound/454 grams frozen bread dough, thawed, at room temperature

1 cup/250 mL whole pitted prunes or mixed dried fruit

Spray cookie sheet with nonstick cooking spray or oil lightly.

Combine 1 cup/250 mL oats and margarine in medium bowl; mix well. Stir in almonds, sugar, 1 tablespoon/15 mL egg substitute and almond extract.

Turn bread dough out onto lightly floured surface. Roll or pat dough into 12×10-inch rectangle. Spread oat mixture in narrow strip down middle; top with prunes. On each side of filling, cut 3-inch diagonal slits 2 inches apart. Fold alternating strips of dough over filling to form a braid pattern, pinching ends of strips to seal. Transfer to cookie sheet. Cover; let rise in warm place 30 minutes or until almost doubled in size.

Heat oven to 350°F/180°C. Brush loaf with remaining 1 tablespoon/15 mL egg substitute; sprinkle with remaining 2 tablespoons/30 mL oats.

Bake 30 to 35 minutes or until golden brown. Serve warm.

MAKES 8 SERVINGS

HONEY
LEMON
TEA LOAVES

1	container (6 ounces/170 grams) low fat or fat-free lemon yogurt
⅔	cup/150 mL double-strength brewed green or black tea, at room temperature
½	cup/125 mL honey
3	tablespoons/45 mL canola oil
1	egg
1½	cups/350 mL **Quaker® 100% Whole Grain Large Flake Oats** or **Quaker® 100% Whole Grain Quick Oats** (uncooked)
1½	cups/350 mL whole wheat flour
1	tablespoon/15 mL grated lemon peel
1	tablespoon/15 mL baking powder
½	teaspoon/2.5 mL baking soda
½	teaspoon/2.5 mL salt

Heat oven to 350°F/180°C. Lightly spray two disposable aluminum foil loaf pans (8½×4-inch or 8×3¾-inch) with nonstick cooking spray.

Combine yogurt, tea, honey, oil and egg with wire whisk or fork in large bowl; mix well. Add oats; mix well. Let stand 10 minutes. Combine flour, lemon peel, baking powder, baking soda and salt in medium bowl; mix well. Add to oat mixture; stir just until dry ingredients are moistened. (Do not overmix.) Pour into prepared pans.

Bake 30 to 35 minutes or until wooden pick inserted in centre comes out with a few moist crumbs clinging to it. Cool completely in pan on wire rack. Store tightly wrapped up to three days. Label and freeze for longer storage.

MAKES 2 LOAVES (12 SERVINGS EACH)

FILLED CRANBERRY WREATHS

WREATHS

- 1 can (16 ounces/454 grams) whole-berry cranberry sauce
- 1 package (16 ounces/454 grams) hot roll mix
- 1 cup/250 mL **Quaker® 100% Whole Grain Large Flake Oats or Quaker® 100% Whole Grain Quick Oats** (uncooked)
- ¼ cup/60 mL granulated sugar
- 1 cup/250 mL hot water (120°F to 130°F/49°C to 55°C)
- ¼ cup/60 mL liquid egg substitute or 1 egg, lightly beaten
- 3 tablespoons/45 mL margarine or butter, softened
- ½ cup/125 mL chopped nuts, divided
- 2 tablespoons/30 mL granulated sugar, divided

ICING

- ¾ cup/175 mL powdered sugar
- 3 to 4 teaspoons/15 mL to 20 mL low fat or fat-free (skim) milk
- ¼ teaspoon/1.25 mL vanilla extract

Spray two cookie sheets with nonstick cooking spray. Place cranberry sauce in fine strainer or sieve; stir to break up. Set aside to drain thoroughly.

Combine contents of box and yeast packet from hot roll mix, oats and ¼ cup/60 mL granulated sugar in large bowl; mix well. Stir in hot water, egg substitute and margarine until dough pulls away from bowl. Knead on lightly floured surface 5 minutes or until smooth. Divide dough in half. Keep half of dough covered. Press other half of dough into 12×8-inch rectangle on one cookie sheet. Top with half of drained cranberry sauce, ¼ cup/60 mL nuts and 1 tablespoon/15 mL granulated sugar to within 1 inch of edge. Roll up, starting from long side, pinching seams and ends to seal. Bring ends together to form ring. With kitchen shears, cut through ring almost to centre at 2-inch intervals. Make second wreath with remaining dough and filling ingredients. Cover both wreaths loosely with plastic wrap; let rise in warm place 30 minutes or until nearly doubled in size.

Heat oven to 350°F/180°C. Uncover wreaths. Bake 23 to 28 minutes or until golden brown. Carefully remove to wire rack.

For icing, combine all ingredients in small bowl; mix until smooth. Spread over top of each wreath. Serve warm or at room temperature.

MAKES 2 WREATHS (12 SERVINGS EACH)

tip

To reheat, microwave at HIGH 15 to 20 seconds per serving.

PEACH STREUSEL COFFEE CAKE

STREUSEL

- ½ cup/125 mL **Quaker® 100% Whole Grain Large Flake Oats or Quaker® 100% Whole Grain Quick Oats** (uncooked)

- ⅓ cup/75 mL granulated sugar

- 3 tablespoons/45 mL margarine, melted

- ½ teaspoon/2.5 mL ground cinnamon

- ⅛ teaspoon/0.625 mL ground nutmeg (optional)

COFFEE CAKE

- 1 cup/250 mL granulated sugar

- ½ cup/125 mL (1 stick) margarine, softened

- 1½ teaspoons/7.5 mL vanilla extract

- 4 egg whites or 2 whole eggs

- 1½ cups/350 mL all-purpose flour

- ¾ cup/175 mL **Quaker® 100% Whole Grain Large Flake Oats or Quaker® 100% Whole Grain Quick Oats** (uncooked)

- 1 tablespoon/15 mL baking powder

- ½ teaspoon/2.5 mL baking soda

- ¾ cup/175 mL light sour cream

- 1 can (16 ounces/454 grams) sliced peaches, drained, or 1 cup/250 mL sliced fresh peaches

Heat oven to 350°F/180°C. Spray 9-inch square baking pan with nonstick cooking spray or grease lightly.

For streusel, combine all ingredients in small bowl; mix until crumbly. Set aside.

For coffee cake, beat 1 cup/250 mL sugar, ½ cup/125 mL margarine and vanilla extract until fluffy. Add egg whites; mix until smooth. Combine flour, ¾ cup/175 mL oats, baking powder and baking soda; mix well. Add to margarine mixture alternately with sour cream, beginning and ending with dry ingredients; mix well after each addition. Spread into prepared pan.

Pat peach slices dry with paper towels; arrange over batter. Sprinkle with streusel.

Bake 50 to 55 minutes or until wooden pick inserted in center comes out with a few moist crumbs clinging to it. Serve warm.

MAKES 16 SERVINGS

VERY BERRY
BREAKFAST
CAKE

STREUSEL

½ cup/125 mL **Quaker® 100% Whole Grain Large Flake Oats** or **Quaker® 100% Whole Grain Quick Oats** (uncooked)

¼ cup/60 mL granulated sugar

3 tablespoons/45 mL margarine or butter, melted

¼ teaspoon/1.25 mL ground cinnamon

CAKE

1 cup/250 mL granulated sugar

½ cup/125 mL (1 stick) margarine or butter, softened

4 egg whites or 2 eggs, lightly beaten

1 container (8 ounces/225 grams) reduced-fat sour cream

1 teaspoon/5 mL vanilla extract

1½ cups/350 mL all-purpose flour

¾ cup/175 mL **Quaker® 100% Whole Grain Large Flake Oats** or **Quaker® 100% Whole Grain Quick Oats** (uncooked)

2 teaspoons/10 mL baking powder

½ teaspoon/2.5 mL baking soda

⅓ cup/75 mL raspberry preserves

¾ cup/175 mL fresh or frozen blueberries

Heat oven to 350°F/180°C. Spray 9-inch square metal baking pan with nonstick cooking spray or grease lightly.

For streusel, combine all ingredients in small bowl; mix well. Set aside.

For cake, beat 1 cup/250 mL sugar and ½ cup/125 mL margarine in large bowl with electric mixer until fluffy. Add egg whites, sour cream and vanilla extract; mix until smooth. Add combined flour, ¾ cup/175 mL oats, baking powder and baking soda; mix just until blended. Spread into prepared pan. Spoon preserves over batter; swirl through batter with knife. Sprinkle blueberries evenly over batter. Sprinkle streusel over blueberries.

Bake 50 to 55 minutes or until wooden pick inserted in centre comes out clean. Serve warm. Store tightly covered at room temperature.

MAKES 12 SERVINGS

PUMPKIN SPICE BREAD

1 cup/250 mL **Quaker® 100% Whole Grain Large Flake Oats** or **Quaker® 100% Whole Grain Quick Oats** (uncooked)

½ cup/125 mL fat-free (skim) milk

1 cup/250 mL all-purpose flour

1 cup/250 mL whole wheat flour

¼ cup/60 mL firmly packed brown sugar

2 teaspoons/10 mL baking powder

2 teaspoons/10 mL pumpkin pie spice

½ teaspoon/2.5 mL baking soda

½ teaspoon/2.5 mL salt

1 cup/250 mL canned pumpkin

2 whole eggs, lightly beaten

¼ cup/60 mL vegetable oil

½ cup/125 mL raisins

tip

To make your own pumpkin pie spice, combine 4 teaspoons/ 20 mL ground cinnamon, 1 teaspoon/5 mL ground ginger, ½ teaspoon/2.5 mL ground allspice, ½ teaspoon/2.5 mL ground cloves and ½ teaspoon/2.5 mL ground nutmeg in a small container with a tight-fitting lid. Store in cool, dark cabinet.

Heat oven to 350°F/180°C. Lightly grease or spray bottom only of two 8×4-inch loaf pans or one 9×5-inch loaf pan with nonstick cooking spray. Combine oats and milk in medium bowl; mix well. Set aside.

Combine all-purpose flour, whole wheat flour, brown sugar, baking powder, pumpkin pie spice, baking soda and salt in large bowl; mix well.

Add pumpkin, eggs, oil and raisins to oat mixture; mix well. Add to dry ingredients all at once; stir just until dry ingredients are moistened. (Do not overmix.) Pour into prepared pans.

Bake 45 to 55 minutes for 8×4-inch pans (55 to 65 minutes for 9×5-inch pan) or until wooden pick inserted in centre comes out clean. Cool 10 minutes in pan; remove to wire rack. Cool completely before slicing. Store tightly wrapped.

MAKES 12 TO 16 SERVINGS

BANANA
PECAN OATMEAL
BREAD

TOPPING

½ cup/125 mL **Quaker® 100% Whole Grain Large Flake Oats** or **Quaker® 100% Whole Grain Quick Oats** (uncooked)

¼ cup/60 mL chopped pecans

1½ tablespoons/22.5 mL margarine or butter, melted

BREAD

1 cup/250 mL **Quaker® 100% Whole Grain Large Flake Oats** or **Quaker® 100% Whole Grain Quick Oats** (uncooked)

½ cup/125 mL fat-free (skim) milk

1 cup/250 mL mashed very ripe bananas (about 3 medium)

⅓ cup/75 mL vegetable oil

2 large eggs, lightly beaten

2 cups/500 mL all-purpose flour

⅓ cup/75 mL granulated sugar

2 teaspoons/10 mL baking powder

1½ teaspoons/7.5 mL ground cinnamon

½ teaspoon/2.5 mL baking soda

½ teaspoon/2.5 mL salt

Heat oven to 350°F/180°C. Spray bottom only of 9×5-inch loaf pan with nonstick cooking spray. Combine all topping ingredients. Set aside.

For bread, combine oats and milk in medium bowl; mix well. Let stand 10 minutes. Add bananas, oil and eggs; mix well.

Combine flour, sugar, baking powder, cinnamon, baking soda and salt in large bowl; mix well. Add oat mixture to dry ingredients all at once; stir just until dry ingredients are moistened. (Do not overmix.) Pour into prepared pan. Sprinkle evenly with reserved topping; pat gently.

Bake 55 to 65 minutes or until wooden pick inserted in centre comes out clean. Cool 10 minutes in pan; remove to wire rack. Cool completely. Store tightly wrapped.

MAKES 12 TO 16 SERVINGS

BREAKFAST ON THE RUN

APPLE RAISIN SCONES

1½ cups/350 mL all-purpose flour

¼ cup/60 mL granulated sugar

1 tablespoon/15 mL baking powder

1 teaspoon/5 mL ground cinnamon

⅓ cup/75 mL (⅔ stick) cold margarine (not vegetable oil spread) or butter

1 cup/250 mL **Quaker® Oat Bran** hot cereal

⅔ cup/150 mL (3 ounces/90 grams) finely chopped dried apples

½ cup/125 mL raisins

½ cup/125 mL water

2 large egg whites, beaten

Jelly, jam or fruit preserves

Heat oven to 400°F/200°C. Lightly spray cookie sheet with nonstick cooking spray or oil lightly.

Combine flour, sugar, baking powder and cinnamon in large bowl; mix well. Cut in margarine with pastry blender or two knives until mixture resembles coarse crumbs. Stir in oat bran, apples and raisins. Combine water and egg whites; add to flour mixture, mixing just until moistened.

Shape dough to form a ball. Turn out onto lightly floured surface; knead gently 6 times. Pat into 9-inch circle on prepared cookie sheet. Score dough into 8 wedges; do not separate.

Bake 18 to 20 minutes or until light golden brown. Break apart. Serve warm with jelly, jam or fruit preserves.

MAKES 8 SCONES

MARVELOUS MORNING MUFFINS

MUFFINS

- 1 cup/250 mL **Quaker® 100% Whole Grain Large Flake Oats or Quaker® 100% Whole Grain Quick Oats** (uncooked)
- 1 cup/250 mL all-purpose flour
- ½ cup/125 mL whole wheat flour
- ⅓ cup/75 mL firmly packed brown sugar
- ½ cup/125 mL raisins
- 1 tablespoon/15 mL baking powder
- 1 teaspoon/5 mL ground cinnamon
- ½ teaspoon/2.5 mL baking soda
- ½ teaspoon/2.5 mL salt
- 1 can (8 ounces/225 grams) crushed pineapple in juice, undrained
- ½ cup/125 mL shredded carrots
- ½ cup/125 mL fat-free (skim) milk
- ⅓ cup/75 mL vegetable oil
- 1 large egg

GLAZE

- 2 tablespoons/30 mL powdered sugar
- 1 teaspoon/5 mL fat-free (skim) milk

Heat oven to 400°F/200°C. Line 12 medium muffin pan cups with paper baking cups or spray bottoms only with nonstick cooking spray.

For muffins, combine oats, all-purpose flour, whole wheat flour, brown sugar, raisins, baking powder, cinnamon, baking soda and salt in large bowl; mix well. Combine pineapple (with juice), carrots, ½ cup/125 mL milk, oil and egg in medium bowl; blend well. Add to dry ingredients all at once; stir just until dry ingredients are moistened. (Do not overmix.) Fill muffin cups almost full.

Bake 20 to 22 minutes or until golden brown. Cool muffins in pan on wire rack 5 minutes. Remove from pan. Cool 10 minutes.

For glaze, combine ingredients in small bowl; mix until smooth. Drizzle evenly over muffins. Serve warm.

MAKES 12 MUFFINS

DOUBLE
ORANGE-WALNUT
MUFFINS

1½ cups/350 mL all-purpose flour*

1 cup/250 mL **Quaker® 100% Whole Grain Large Flake Oats** or **Quaker® 100% Whole Grain Quick Oats** (uncooked)

⅔ cup plus 1 tablespoon/165 mL granulated sugar, divided

2 teaspoons/10 mL baking powder

½ teaspoon/2.5 mL baking soda

¼ teaspoon/1.25 mL salt

¾ cup/175 mL coarsely chopped toasted walnuts, divided

⅔ cup plus ¼ cup/210 mL **Tropicana Pure Premium®** orange juice, divided

½ cup/125 mL low fat (1%) or fat-free (skim) milk

1 large egg

¼ cup/60 mL (½ stick) butter or margarine, melted and cooled

*If using large flake oats, add 2 tablespoons/30 mL additional flour.

tip

Chopped toasted pecans may be substituted for walnuts. Nuts may be omitted, if desired.

Heat oven to 400°F/200°C. Line 12 medium muffin pan cups with paper baking cups or spray bottoms only with nonstick cooking spray.

Combine flour, oats, ⅔ cup/150 mL sugar, baking powder, baking soda and salt in large bowl. Add ½ cup/125 mL walnuts; mix well. Set aside. Beat ⅔ cup/150 mL juice, milk, egg and butter with whisk or fork in medium bowl until well blended. Add to dry ingredients all at once; stir just until dry ingredients are moistened. (Do not overmix.) Pour into muffin cups, dividing evenly. Sprinkle tops with remaining ¼ cup/60 mL walnuts.

Bake 15 to 18 minutes or until wooden pick inserted in centres comes out clean. Remove pan from oven and immediately spoon remaining ¼ cup/ 60 mL orange juice over muffin tops, dividing evenly. Let stand 5 minutes. Sprinkle muffin tops with remaining 1 tablespoon/15 mL sugar. Remove from pan. Serve warm.

MAKES 12 MUFFINS

FRUIT
AND OAT
SCONES

1½ cups/350 mL all-purpose flour

1 cup/250 mL **Quaker® 100% Whole Grain Large Flake Oats** or **Quaker® 100% Whole Grain Quick Oats** (uncooked)

Heat-stable sugar substitute equal to 3 tablespoons/45 mL sugar

1½ teaspoons/7.5 mL baking powder

½ teaspoon/2.5 mL baking soda

½ teaspoon/2.5 mL ground cinnamon

¼ teaspoon/1.25 mL salt (optional)

5 tablespoons/75 mL margarine, chilled and cut into pieces

⅓ cup/75 mL finely chopped dried mixed fruit, dried cranberries or raisins

⅔ cup/150 mL low fat buttermilk

¼ cup/60 mL liquid egg substitute or 2 egg whites, lightly beaten

tip

If buttermilk is unavailable, substitute soured milk. Combine 2 teaspoons/10 mL vinegar or lemon juice with enough milk to equal ⅔ cup/150 mL. Stir well. Let stand 5 minutes before using.

Heat oven to 400°F/200°C. Lightly spray cookie sheet with nonstick cooking spray.

Combine flour, oats, sweetener, baking powder, baking soda, cinnamon and, if desired, salt in large bowl; mix well. Cut in margarine with pastry blender or two knives until mixture resembles coarse crumbs. Stir in dried fruit. Add combined buttermilk and egg substitute to flour mixture all at once; stir just until dry ingredients are moistened. (Do not overmix.) Drop dough by ¼-cup/60-mL portions 2 inches apart onto cookie sheet.

Bake 12 to 15 minutes or until very light golden brown. Serve warm.

MAKES 10 SCONES

MULTI-GRAIN
APRICOT OAT
MUFFINS

1 cup/250 mL **Quaker® 100% Whole Grain Large Flake Oats** or **Quaker® 100% Whole Grain Quick Oats** (uncooked)

1 cup/250 mL whole wheat flour*

½ cup/125 mL firmly packed brown sugar

⅓ cup/75 mL **Quaker® Kretschmer® Original Toasted Wheat Germ**

2 teaspoons/10 mL baking powder

1½ teaspoons/7.5 mL grated orange peel

1 teaspoon/5 mL ground cinnamon

½ teaspoon/2.5 mL salt

1 cup/250 mL fat-free (skim) milk

2 egg whites, lightly beaten

¼ cup/60 mL vegetable oil

¼ cup/60 mL apricot fruit spread, plus additional for glaze

Additional oats, for topping

*If using large flake oats, add 2 tablespoons/30 mL additional flour.

Heat oven to 400°F/200°C. Line 12 medium muffin pan cups with paper baking cups.

Combine oats, whole wheat flour, brown sugar, wheat germ, baking powder, orange peel, cinnamon and salt in large bowl; mix well. Combine milk, egg whites and oil; mix well. Add to dry ingredients all at once; stir just until blended. (Batter will be thin.)

Fill muffin cups ⅓ full with batter. Carefully spoon 1 teaspoon/5 mL apricot fruit spread into centre of each muffin cup. Spoon remaining batter over fruit spread, dividing evenly. Sprinkle each filled muffin cup with additional oats.

Bake 20 to 22 minutes or until golden brown. Remove from oven to wire rack. Lightly brush additional fruit spread onto warm muffin tops to glaze. Let stand 10 minutes. Remove from pan. Serve warm.

MAKES 12 MUFFINS

tip

To freeze, wrap cooled muffins securely in foil, or place in freezer bag. Seal, label and freeze up to six months.

CINNAMON
BUN
SCONES

2   cups/500 mL all-purpose flour

1   cup/250 mL **Quaker® 100% Whole Grain Large Flake Oats** or **Quaker® 100% Whole Grain Quick Oats** (uncooked)

¼   cup plus 2 tablespoons/90 mL granulated sugar, divided

1   tablespoon/15 mL baking powder

¼   teaspoon/1.25 mL salt

½   cup/125 mL (1 stick) butter, chilled and cut into pieces

¾   cup/175 mL whole or low fat (2%) milk

1   egg, lightly beaten

1   teaspoon/5 mL vanilla extract

½   cup/125 mL toasted chopped pecans

2   teaspoons/10 mL ground cinnamon

¾   cup/175 mL powdered sugar

3   to 4 teaspoons/15 to 20 mL **Tropicana Pure Premium®** orange juice or milk

Heat oven to 425°F/220°C. Spray cookie sheet with nonstick cooking spray.

Combine flour, oats, ¼ cup/60 mL granulated sugar, baking powder and salt in large bowl; mix well. Cut in butter with pastry blender or two knives until mixture resembles coarse crumbs. Combine milk, egg and vanilla extract in small bowl; blend well. Add to dry ingredients all at once; stir with fork or rubber spatula just until dry ingredients are moistened. (Do not overmix.)

Combine remaining 2 tablespoons/30 mL granulated sugar with pecans and cinnamon in small bowl; mix well. Sprinkle evenly over dough in bowl; gently stir batter to swirl in cinnamon mixture. (Do not blend completely.) Drop dough by ¼-cup/60-mL portions 2 inches apart on cookie sheet.

Bake 11 to 13 minutes or until golden brown. Remove to wire rack; cool 5 minutes.

Combine powdered sugar and enough orange juice for desired consistency in small bowl; mix until smooth. Drizzle over warm scones. Serve warm.

MAKES 12 SCONES

COCOA
BANANA MINI
MUFFINS

1¼	cups/300 mL all-purpose flour
1	cup/250 mL **Quaker® 100% Whole Grain Large Flake Oats** or **Quaker® 100% Whole Grain Quick Oats** (uncooked)
½	cup/125 mL granulated sugar
⅓	cup/75 mL unsweetened cocoa powder
2	teaspoons/10 mL baking powder
¼	teaspoon/1.25 mL baking soda
⅔	cup/150 mL mashed ripe bananas (about 2 small)
½	cup/125 mL fat-free (skim) milk
5	tablespoons/75 mL margarine or butter, melted
2	egg whites or 1 egg, lightly beaten
1	teaspoon/5 mL vanilla extract
	Powdered sugar (optional)

Heat oven to 400°F/200°C. Line 36 miniature muffin pan cups with paper baking cups or spray bottoms only with nonstick cooking spray.

Combine flour, oats, granulated sugar, cocoa, baking powder and baking soda in large bowl; mix well. Combine bananas, milk, margarine, egg whites and vanilla extract in medium bowl; blend well. Add to dry ingredients all at once; stir just until dry ingredients are moistened. (Do not overmix.) Fill muffin cups almost full.

Bake 10 to 12 minutes or until wooden pick inserted in centres comes out clean. Cool muffins in pan on wire rack 5 minutes. Remove from pan. Cool completely.

Sprinkle with powdered sugar, if desired. Store tightly covered.

MAKES 36 MINIATURE MUFFINS

PUMPKIN
OAT STREUSEL
MUFFINS

STREUSEL

- ¼ cup/60 mL **Large Flake Quaker®
  Oats** or **Quick Quaker® Oats**
  (uncooked)

- 1 tablespoon/15 mL firmly
  packed brown sugar

- 1 tablespoon/15 mL margarine
  or butter, melted

- ⅛ teaspoon/0.625 mL pumpkin
  pie spice

MUFFINS

- 1½ cups/350 mL all-purpose flour

- 1 cup/250 mL **Quaker® 100%
  Whole Grain Large Flake
  Oats** or **Quaker® 100%
  Whole Grain Quick Oats**
  (uncooked)

- ¾ cup/175 mL firmly packed
  brown sugar

- ½ cup/125 mL chopped nuts
  (optional)

- 1 Tablespoon/15 mL baking
  powder

- 1½ teaspoons/7.5 mL pumpkin pie
  spice

- ½ teaspoon/2.5 mL baking soda

- ½ teaspoon/2.5 mL salt (optional)

- 1 cup/250 mL canned pumpkin

- ¾ cup/175 mL milk

- ⅓ cup/75 mL vegetable oil

- 1 egg, lightly beaten

Heat oven to 400°F/200°C. Line 12 medium muffin pan cups with paper baking cups or spray bottoms only with nonstick cooking spray.

For streusel, combine oats, brown sugar, margarine and pumpkin pie spice in small bowl; mix well. Set aside.

For muffins, combine flour, oats, brown sugar, nuts, if desired, baking powder, pumpkin pie spice, baking soda and salt, if desired, in large bowl; mix well. Combine pumpkin, milk, oil and egg in medium bowl; blend well. Add to dry ingredients all at once; stir just until dry ingredients are moistened. (Do not overmix.) Fill muffin cups almost full. Sprinkle with reserved streusel, patting gently.

Bake 22 to 25 minutes or until golden brown. Cool muffins in pan on wire rack 5 minutes. Remove from pan. Serve warm.

MAKES 12 MUFFINS

APPLE 'N' CHEDDAR OATMEAL MUFFINS

1¼ cups/300 mL **Quaker® 100% Whole Grain Large Flake Oats** or **Quaker® 100% Whole Grain Quick Oats** (uncooked)

1¼ cups/300 mL all-purpose flour

½ cup/125 mL granulated sugar

1 teaspoon/5 mL baking powder

1 teaspoon/5 mL apple pie spice or ground cinnamon

½ teaspoon/2.5 mL baking soda

¼ teaspoon/1.25 mL salt (optional)

¾ cup/175 mL chopped apple (about 1 medium)

¾ cup/175 mL (3 ounces/90 grams) shredded reduced-fat Cheddar cheese

1 cup/250 mL apple juice or fat-free (skim) milk

2 egg whites or 1 egg, slightly beaten

2 tablespoons/30 mL vegetable oil

Heat oven to 400°F/200°C. Line 12 medium muffin pan cups with paper baking cups or spray bottoms only with nonstick cooking spray.

Combine oats, flour, sugar, baking powder, apple pie spice, baking soda and, if desired, salt; mix well. Stir in apple and Cheddar cheese. Add combined apple juice, egg whites and oil; mix just until dry ingredients are moistened. Fill muffin cups almost full.

Bake 20 to 24 minutes or until golden brown. Cool muffins in pan on wire rack 5 minutes. Remove from pan. Serve warm.

MAKES 12 MUFFINS

LEMON
BLUEBERRY OATMEAL
MUFFINS

TOPPING

- ¼ cup/60 mL **Quaker® 100% Whole Grain Large Flake Oats** or **Quaker® 100% Whole Grain Quick Oats** (uncooked)
- 2 tablespoons/30 mL firmly packed brown sugar

MUFFINS

- 1½ cups/350 mL **Quaker® 100% Whole Grain Large Flake Oats** or **Quaker® 100% Whole Grain Quick Oats** (uncooked)
- 1 cup/250 mL all-purpose flour*
- ½ cup/125 mL granulated sugar
- 1 tablespoon/15 mL baking powder
- ¼ teaspoon/1.25 mL salt (optional)
- 1 cup/250 mL fat free (skim) milk
- 2 egg whites or ¼ cup/60 mL liquid egg substitute with yolk or 1 egg
- 2 tablespoons/30 mL canola oil
- 1 teaspoon/5 mL grated lemon peel
- 1 teaspoon/5 mL vanilla extract
- 1 cup/250 mL fresh or frozen blueberries (do not thaw)

*If using large flake oats, add 2 tablespoons/30 mL additional flour.

Heat oven to 400°F/200°C. Spray 12 medium muffin pan cups with nonstick cooking spray.

For topping, combine ingredients in small bowl. Set aside.

For muffins, combine 1½ cups/350 mL oats, flour, granulated sugar, baking powder and, if desired, salt in large bowl; mix well. Combine milk, egg whites, oil, lemon peel and vanilla extract in small bowl; mix well. Add to dry ingredients all at once; stir just until dry ingredients are moistened. (Do not overmix.) Gently stir in berries. Fill muffin cups almost full; sprinkle with topping.

Bake 18 to 22 minutes or until light golden brown. Cool muffins in pan on wire rack 5 minutes. Remove from pan. Serve warm.

MAKES 12 MUFFINS

APPLESAUCE
OATMEAL
MUFFINS

TOPPING

¼ cup/60 mL **Quaker® 100% Whole Grain Large Flake Oats** or **Quaker® 100% Whole Grain Quick Oats** (uncooked)

1 tablespoon/15 mL firmly packed brown sugar

1 tablespoon/15 mL light butter or butter, melted

¼ teaspoon/1.25 mL ground cinnamon

MUFFINS

1½ cups/350 mL **Quaker® 100% Whole Grain Large Flake Oats** or **Quaker® 100% Whole Grain Quick Oats** (uncooked)

1¼ cups/300 mL all-purpose flour

1 teaspoon/5 mL baking powder

¾ teaspoon/3.75 mL baking soda

¾ teaspoon/3.75 mL ground cinnamon

1 cup/250 mL unsweetened applesauce

½ cup/125 mL fat-free (skim) milk

⅓ cup/75 mL firmly packed brown sugar

3 tablespoons/45 mL canola oil

¼ cup/60 mL liquid egg substitute with yolk or 1 egg, lightly beaten

Heat oven to 400°F/200°C. Line 12 medium muffin pan cups with paper baking cups or spray bottoms only with nonstick cooking spray.

For topping, combine all ingredients in small bowl; mix well. Set aside.

For muffins, combine 1½ cups/350 mL oats, flour, baking powder, baking soda and ¾ teaspoon/3.75 mL cinnamon in large bowl; mix well. Combine applesauce, milk, ⅓ cup/75 mL brown sugar, oil and egg substitute in medium bowl; blend well. Add to dry ingredients all at once; stir just until dry ingredients are moistened. (Do not overmix.) Fill muffin cups almost full. Sprinkle with reserved topping, patting gently.

Bake 20 to 22 minutes or until golden brown. Cool muffins in pan on wire rack 5 minutes. Remove from pan. Serve warm.

MAKES 12 MUFFINS

WARM
PRALINES 'N' CREAM
MUFFINS

1 cup/250 mL **Quaker® 100% Whole Grain Large Flake Oats** or **Quaker® 100% Whole Grain Quick Oats** (uncooked)

½ cup/125 mL all-purpose flour

⅓ cup/75 mL whole wheat flour

1 tablespoon/15 mL baking powder

½ teaspoon/2.5 mL salt

¾ cup/175 mL chopped pecans, divided

½ cup/125 mL firmly packed brown sugar

⅓ cup/75 mL (⅔ stick) margarine or butter, softened

1 package (3 ounces/90 grams) cream cheese, softened

⅔ cup/150 mL milk

1 egg

1 teaspoon/5 mL maple extract or vanilla extract

Heat oven to 400°F/200°C. Line 12 medium muffin pan cups with paper baking cups.

Combine oats, all-purpose flour, whole wheat flour, baking powder, salt and ½ cup/125 mL pecans in medium bowl; mix well. Beat brown sugar, margarine and cream cheese in separate bowl until creamy. Add milk, egg and maple extract; mix well. Add to dry ingredients all at once; stir just until dry ingredients are moistened. (Do not overmix.) Fill muffin cups ¾ full. Sprinkle with remaining ¼ cup/60 mL pecans.

Bake 20 to 22 minutes or until golden brown. Cool muffins in pan on wire rack 5 minutes. Remove from pan.

MAKES 12 MUFFINS

tip

To freeze muffins, wrap securely; seal, label and freeze. To reheat frozen muffins, unwrap muffins; microwave on HIGH about 45 seconds per muffin.

OATMEAL
DROP
BISCUITS

1¼ cups/300 mL **Quaker® 100% Whole Grain Large Flake Oats** or **Quaker® 100% Whole Grain Quick Oats** (uncooked)

¾ cup/175 mL all-purpose flour

2 tablespoons/30 mL granulated sugar

1 teaspoon/5 mL baking powder

½ teaspoon/2.5 mL baking soda

¼ teaspoon/1.25 mL salt

¼ cup/60 mL (½ stick) margarine, chilled and cut into pieces

1¾ cups/450 mL low fat buttermilk

¼ cup/60 mL vegetable oil

¾ cup/175 mL raisins

Heat oven to 450°F/230°C.

Combine oats, flour, sugar, baking powder, baking soda and salt in large bowl; mix well. Cut in margarine with pastry blender or two knives until mixture resembles coarse crumbs. Add buttermilk and oil; stir with fork just until dry ingredients are moistened. Add raisins; mix just until blended. (Do not overmix.) Drop dough by ¼-cup/60-mL portions 2 inches apart onto ungreased cookie sheets.

Bake 10 to 12 minutes or until light golden brown. Serve warm.

MAKES 16 SERVINGS

tip

If buttermilk is unavailable, substitute soured milk. Combine 4 teaspoons/20 mL vinegar or lemon juice with enough milk to equal 1¾ cups/450 mL. Stir well. Let stand 5 minutes before using.

CRANBERRY
GINGER OAT
SCONES

1⅓ cups/325 mL all-purpose flour

1 cup/250 mL **Quaker® 100% Whole Grain Large Flake Oats** or **Quaker® 100% Whole Grain Quick Oats** (uncooked)

¼ cup plus 1 tablespoon/75 mL granulated sugar, divided

2 teaspoons/10 mL baking powder

1 teaspoon/5 mL ground ginger

½ teaspoon/2.5 mL baking soda

½ teaspoon/2.5 mL salt

½ cup/125 mL (1 stick) butter or margarine, chilled and cut into pieces

¾ cup/175 mL sweetened dried cranberries

⅓ cup/75 mL fat-free plain yogurt

1 egg

Heat oven to 400°F/200°C.

Combine flour, oats, ¼ cup/60 mL sugar, baking powder, ginger, baking soda and salt in large bowl; mix well. Work butter into dry ingredients with fork or fingertips until mixture resembles small peas. Stir in cranberries. Combine yogurt and egg in small bowl; blend well. Add to dry ingredients all at once; stir with fork until soft dough forms.

Turn dough out onto floured surface, knead gently 8 to 10 times. Transfer to ungreased cookie sheet. Pat into 8-inch diameter circle; sprinkle with remaining 1 tablespoon/15 mL sugar. Cut into eight wedges; separate wedges slightly.

Bake 12 to 14 minutes or until light golden brown. Separate wedges; transfer to cooling rack. Serve warm.

MAKES 8 SCONES

tip

For biscuits and scones that are light, tender and flaky, cut chilled butter or margarine into dry ingredients until particles are the size of coarse crumbs. After adding liquids, handle dough as gently and as little as possible.

CINNAMON
COFFEE CAKE
MUFFINS

TOPPING

¼ cup/60 mL **Large Flake Quaker®
Oats or Quick Quaker® Oats**
(uncooked)

3 tablespoons/45 mL whole
wheat flour

2 tablespoons/30 mL
granulated sugar

1 tablespoon/15 mL trans
fat-free spread

¼ teaspoon/1.25 mL ground
cinnamon

MUFFINS

3 tablespoons plus ½ cup/170 mL granulated sugar, divided

1 tablespoon/15 mL ground cinnamon

1 cup/250 mL **Quaker® 100% Whole Grain Large Flake Oats** or
Quaker® 100% Whole Grain Quick Oats (uncooked)

1 cup/250 mL low fat buttermilk

1 egg, well beaten

¼ cup/60 mL canola oil

½ cup/125 mL all-purpose flour*

½ cup/125 mL whole wheat flour

¼ cup/60 mL **Quaker® Kretschmer® Original Toasted Wheat Germ**

1½ teaspoons/7.5 mL baking powder

½ teaspoon/2.5 mL baking soda

If using large flake oats, add 1 tablespoon/15 mL additional all-purpose flour.

Heat oven to 375°F/190°C. Spray bottoms only of 12 medium muffin pan cups with nonstick cooking spray.

For topping, combine all ingredients in small bowl. Set aside.

For muffins, combine 3 tablespoons/45 mL sugar and 1 tablespoon/15 mL cinnamon in small bowl. Set aside. Combine 1 cup/250 mL oats and buttermilk in large bowl; mix well. Let stand 5 minutes. Stir in egg and oil until blended.

Combine all-purpose flour, ½ cup/125 mL whole wheat flour, wheat germ, baking powder, baking soda and remaining ½ cup/125 mL sugar in medium bowl; mix well. Add to oat mixture all at once; stir just until dry ingredients are moistened. (Do not overmix.) Sprinkle cinnamon-sugar over top of batter; gently stir 4 to 5 times to make swirls. Fill muffin cups almost full; sprinkle with topping.

Bake 18 to 20 minutes or until light golden brown. Cool muffins in pan on wire rack 5 minutes. Serve warm.

MAKES 12 MUFFINS

If buttermilk is unavailable, substitute soured milk. Combine 1 tablespoon/15 mL vinegar or lemon juice with enough milk to equal 1 cup/250 mL. Stir well. Let stand 5 minutes before using.

QUAKER'S
BEST OATMEAL
MUFFINS

STREUSEL

⅓ cup/75 mL **Quaker® 100% Whole Grain Large Flake Oats** or **Quaker® 100% Whole Grain Quick Oats** (uncooked)

¼ cup/60 mL all-purpose flour

¼ cup/60 mL firmly packed brown sugar

3 tablespoons/45 mL butter or light butter, chilled and cut into pieces

MUFFINS

1½ cups/350 mL all-purpose flour

1 cup/250 mL **Quaker® 100% Whole Grain Large Flake Oats** or **Quaker® 100% Whole Grain Quick Oats** (uncooked)

½ cup/125 mL granulated sugar

1 tablespoon/15 mL baking powder

1 cup/250 mL fat-free (skim) milk

¼ cup/60 mL vegetable oil

1 egg, lightly beaten

1 teaspoon/5 mL vanilla extract

Heat oven to 400°F/200°C. Line 12 medium muffin pan cups with paper baking cups or spray bottoms only with nonstick cooking spray.

For streusel, combine ⅓ cup/75 mL oats, ¼ cup/60 mL flour and brown sugar in small bowl; mix well. Cut in butter with pastry blender or two knives until mixture is crumbly. Set aside.

For muffins, combine 1½ cups/350 mL flour, 1 cup/250 mL oats, granulated sugar and baking powder in large bowl; mix well. Combine milk, oil, egg and vanilla extract in small bowl; blend well. Add to dry ingredients all at once; stir just until dry ingredients are moistened. (Do not overmix.) Fill muffin cups almost full. Sprinkle with reserved streusel, patting gently.

Bake 18 to 20 minutes or until golden brown. Cool muffins in pan on wire rack 5 minutes. Remove from pan. Serve warm.

MAKES 12 MUFFINS

WHOLE GRAIN
BANANA
MUFFINS

1½ cups/350 mL all-purpose flour

1 cup/250 mL **Quaker® 100% Whole Grain Large Flake Oats** or **Quaker® 100% Whole Grain Quick Oats** (uncooked)

½ cup/125 mL firmly packed brown sugar

½ cup/125 mL chopped nuts (optional)

1 tablespoon/15 mL baking powder

½ teaspoon/2.5 mL baking soda

1 cup/250 mL mashed ripe bananas (about 3 medium)

½ cup/125 mL fat-free (skim) milk

5 tablespoons/75 mL margarine or butter, melted

2 egg whites or 1 egg, lightly beaten

Heat oven to 400°F/200°C. Line 12 medium muffin pan cups with paper baking cups or spray bottoms only with nonstick cooking spray.

Combine flour, oats, brown sugar, nuts, if desired, baking powder and baking soda in large bowl; mix well. Combine bananas, milk, margarine and egg whites in medium bowl; blend well. Add to dry ingredients all at once; stir just until dry ingredients are moistened. (Do not overmix.) Fill muffin cups almost full.

Bake 17 to 19 minutes or until golden brown. Cool muffins in pan on wire rack 5 minutes. Remove from pan. Serve warm.

MAKES 12 MUFFINS

BLUEBERRY-
GINGER MUFFIN
TOPS

1½ cups/350 mL **Quaker® 100% Whole Grain Large Flake Oats or Quaker® 100% Whole Grain Quick Oats** (uncooked)

½ cup/125 mL granulated sugar

⅓ cup/75 mL (⅔ stick) margarine or butter, melted, divided

1⅓ cups/325 mL all-purpose flour

1 tablespoon/15 mL baking powder

¾ teaspoon/3.75 mL ground ginger

⅔ cup/150 mL milk

1 egg, lightly beaten

1 cup/250 mL blueberries, fresh or frozen

Heat oven to 400°F/200°C. Lightly grease large cookie sheet.

Combine oats and sugar in large bowl; mix well. For streusel topping, combine ¼ cup/ 60 mL oat mixture and 1 tablespoon/15 mL melted margarine in small bowl. Set aside.

For muffins, add flour, baking powder and ginger to remaining oat mixture; mix well. Combine milk, remaining melted margarine and egg in small bowl; mix well. Add to dry ingredients all at once; stir just until dry ingredients are moistened. Stir in blueberries. For each muffin top, drop batter by ¼-cup/60-mL portions onto prepared cookie sheet. Sprinkle streusel topping evenly over batter, patting gently.

Bake 20 to 22 minutes or until golden brown. Serve warm.

MAKES 12 MUFFIN TOPS

tip

To freeze, wrap muffin tops securely in foil, or place in freezer bag; label and freeze. To reheat, microwave on HIGH about 30 seconds per muffin top.

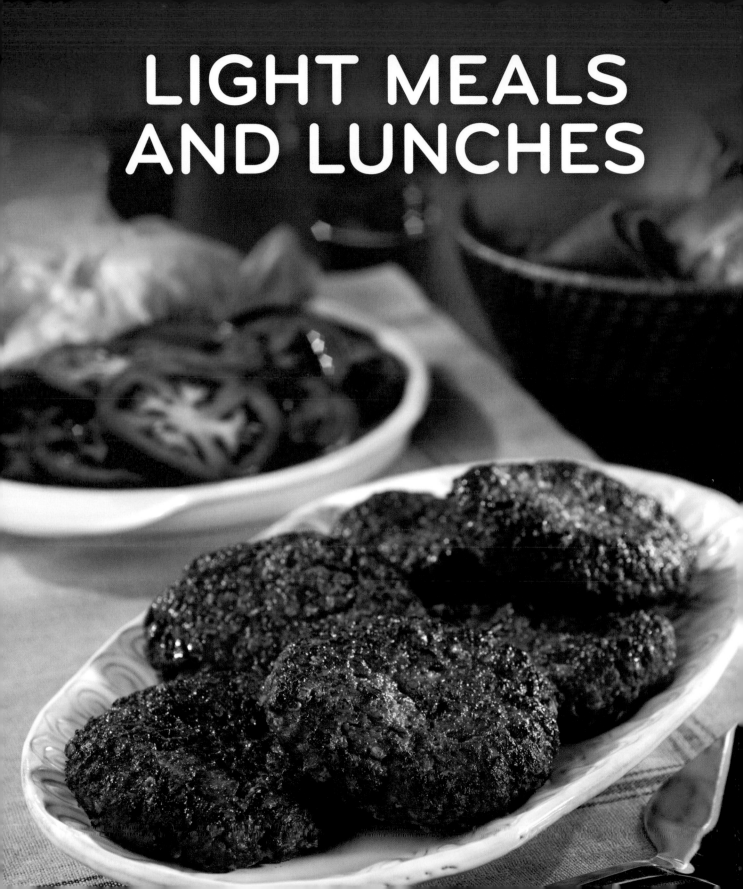

LIGHT MEALS
AND LUNCHES

JUICY JUMBO BURGERS

1   pound/454 grams lean ground beef

½   cup/125 mL **Quaker® 100% Whole Grain Quick Oats** or **Quaker® 100% Whole Grain Large Flake Oats** (uncooked)

1   egg, lightly beaten

½   cup/125 mL ketchup, tomato sauce, beer, barbecue sauce or salsa

1   tablespoon/15 mL finely chopped onion

2   teaspoons/10 mL prepared mustard

½   teaspoon/2.5 mL salt (optional)

⅛   teaspoon/0.625 mL black pepper

     Hamburger buns (optional)

Combine all ingredients except hamburger buns in medium bowl, mixing lightly but thoroughly. Shape into six ½-inch-thick patties.

Broil or pan-fry patties 4 to 6 minutes on each side to medium (160°F/71°C) doneness until no longer pink in centre and juices show no pink colour. Serve on hamburger buns, if desired.

MAKES 6 SERVINGS

QUAKER'S OATMEAL SOUP

1   onion, finely chopped (about ¾ cup/175 mL)

½   cup/125 mL shredded carrots

3   tablespoons/45 mL butter or margarine, divided

½   cup/125 mL **Quaker® 100% Whole Grain Large Flake Oats** or **Quaker® 100% Whole Grain Quick Oats** (uncooked)

6   cups/1.5 litres chicken broth

1   cup/250 mL **Quaker® 100% Whole Grain Large Flake Oats** or **Quaker® 100% Whole Grain Quick Oats,** cooked according to package directions

Salt and black pepper, to taste

3   tablespoons/45 mL finely chopped fresh parsley or 1 tablespoon/15 mL dried parsley flakes

Cook onion and carrots in 2 tablespoons/30 mL butter in large skillet or saucepan over medium-low heat, stirring often, 5 minutes or until onion is tender.

Add ½ cup/125 mL uncooked oats and remaining 1 tablespoon/15 mL butter. Cook, stirring often, 3 minutes or until oats are golden brown.

Stir in broth; bring to a low boil. Add 1 cup/250 mL cooked oatmeal, stirring until well mixed. Cook over medium heat 5 minutes. Season to taste with salt and pepper. Serve sprinkled with parsley.

MAKES 4 SERVINGS

VEGGIE BURGERS

3 teaspoons/15 mL vegetable oil, divided

1 cup/250 mL sliced mushrooms

1 cup/250 mL shredded carrots (about 2)

¾ cup/175 mL chopped onion (about 1 medium)

¾ cup/175 mL chopped zucchini (about 1 small)

2 cups/500 mL **Quaker® 100% Whole Grain Large Flake Oats** or **Quaker® 100% Whole Grain Quick Oats** (uncooked)

1 can (15 ounces/425 grams) kidney beans, rinsed and drained

1 cup/250 mL cooked white or brown rice

2 tablespoons/30 mL soy sauce or ½ teaspoon/2.5 mL salt

1 teaspoon/5 mL minced garlic

⅛ teaspoon/0.625 mL black pepper

½ cup/125 mL chopped fresh cilantro or chives (optional)

Hamburger buns and toppings (optional)

Heat 1 teaspoon/5 mL oil in large nonstick skillet. Add mushrooms, carrots, onion and zucchini; cook over medium-high heat 5 minutes or until vegetables are tender.

Transfer vegetables to food processor bowl. Add oats, beans, rice, soy sauce, garlic, pepper and, if desired, cilantro. Pulse about 20 seconds or until well blended. Divide into eight ½-cup/125-ml portions. Shape into patties between waxed paper. Refrigerate at least 1 hour or until firm.

Heat remaining 2 teaspoons/10 mL oil in same skillet over medium-high heat. Cook patties 3 to 4 minutes on each side or until golden brown. Serve on buns with toppings, if desired.

MAKES 8 SERVINGS

ABC MEATBALL SOUP

MEATBALLS

- 1 pound/454 grams ground turkey breast or extra lean ground beef
- ¾ cup/175 mL **Quaker® 100% Whole Grain Large Flake Oats** or **Quaker® 100% Whole Grain Quick Oats** (uncooked)
- ⅓ cup/75 mL barbecue sauce or ketchup

SOUP

- 1 carton (48 ounces/1.5 litres) reduced-sodium fat-free chicken broth (about 6 cups/1.5 litres)
- ¼ cup/60 mL alphabet or other small shaped pasta
- 1 package (10 ounces/285 grams) frozen mixed vegetables (do not thaw)

Heat broiler. Lightly spray rack of broiler pan with nonstick cooking spray.

For meatballs, combine turkey, oats and barbecue sauce in large bowl; mix lightly but thoroughly. Transfer to sheet of foil. Pat mixture into 9×6-inch rectangle. Cut into 1½-inch squares; roll each square into ball to make 24 meatballs. Arrange on broiler pan.

Broil 6 to 8 inches from heat about 6 minutes or until cooked through, turning once.

For soup, bring chicken broth to a boil in 4-quart/4-litre saucepan or Dutch oven over medium-high heat. Add pasta and frozen vegetables; return to a boil. Reduce heat; cover and simmer 8 minutes or until vegetables and pasta are tender. Add meatballs; cook 1 minute. Serve immediately.

MAKES 6 SERVINGS

tips

Garlic powder, onion powder or dried thyme may be added to the meatball ingredients.

Frozen corn, frozen green beans, frozen peas and carrots, or your favorite vegetable blend may be substituted for the mixed vegetables.

STUFFED TURKEY
BURGERS
WITH SMOKY AÏOLI

AÏOLI

½ cup/125 mL fat-free or reduced-fat mayonnaise

1 canned chipotle pepper in adobo sauce, seeded, minced

¾ teaspoon/3.75 mL adobo sauce (from can above)

1 clove garlic, minced

BURGERS

1½ pounds/680 grams lean ground turkey

1 cup/250 mL **Quaker® 100% Whole Grain Large Flake Oats
or Quaker® 100% Whole Grain Quick Oats** (uncooked)

3 cloves garlic, minced

2 tablespoons/30 mL Worcestershire sauce

1½ teaspoons/7.5 mL dried oregano leaves

1 teaspoon/5 mL salt

½ teaspoon/2.5 mL black pepper

6 fresh mozzarella balls (⅓ to ½ ounce/9 to 14 grams each)

6 whole wheat hamburger buns, split and lightly toasted

¾ cup/175 mL jarred roasted red pepper halves, drained

1 bunch watercress, arugula or other favorite salad greens, stems removed

For aïoli, combine mayonnaise, chipotle pepper, adobo sauce and garlic in small bowl; mix well. Chill at least 30 minutes.

Heat grill or broiler.

For burgers, combine turkey, oats, garlic, Worcestershire sauce, oregano, salt and pepper in large bowl; mix lightly but thoroughly. Shape into six large ¼-inch-thick patties. Place 1 mozzarella ball in centre of each patty; shape burger mixture around cheese to completely enclose; reshape into patty.

Grill or broil 4 inches from heat 5 minutes on each side or until centres are no longer pink (170°F/77°C). Arrange burgers on bottom halves of buns; top with aïoli, roasted pepper pieces, watercress and bun tops.

MAKES 6 SERVINGS

> ## *tip*
>
> *It small fresh mozzarella balls are unavailable, substitute large fresh mozzarella balls, cut into ⅓- to ½-ounce/9- to 14-gram pieces. A 3-ounce/90-gram chunk of part-skim mozzarella cheese, cut into six pieces, can be substituted for fresh mozzarella.*

BACON
CHEESEBURGER
MEATLOAF

MEATLOAF

1½ pounds/680 grams 85% lean ground beef

1 cup/250 mL **Quaker® 100% Whole Grain Large Flake Oats** or **Quaker® 100% Whole Grain Quick Oats** (uncooked)

1 can (8 ounces/225 grams) tomato sauce

¼ cup/60 mL finely chopped onion

1 egg, lightly beaten

½ teaspoon/2.5 mL black pepper

SECRET SAUCE

⅓ cup/75 mL mayonnaise

2 tablespoons/30 mL ketchup

TOPPINGS

8 large slices Cheddar cheese

8 strips thick-sliced bacon, crisp-cooked and cut in half

2 medium tomatoes, sliced

8 hamburger buns or other favorite roll or bread, split and toasted (optional)

Heat oven to 350°F/180°C. Spray 13×9-inch metal baking pan with nonstick cooking spray.

For meatloaf, combine ground beef, oats, tomato sauce, onion, egg and pepper in large bowl; mix lightly but thoroughly. Press mixture into pan.

Bake 30 to 35 minutes to medium doneness (160°F/71°C) until no longer pink in centre and juices show no pink colour. Drain off any juices. Heat broiler.

For secret sauce, combine ingredients in small bowl; mix well. Spread over hot meatloaf, completely covering; cut meatloaf into eight rectangles. (Do not remove from pan.) Top each rectangle with cheese, 2 bacon pieces and tomato slices.

Broil meatloaf 5 to 6 inches from heat source 2 to 3 minutes or until cheese melts. Serve on bun or bread, if desired.

MAKES 8 SERVINGS

SHANGHAI
MEATBALL
SOUP

MEATBALLS

1 pound/454 grams ground turkey

¾ cup/175 mL **Quaker® 100% Whole Grain Large Flake Oats or Quaker® 100% Whole Grain Quick Oats** (uncooked)

¼ cup/60 mL reduced-sodium chicken broth

2 tablespoons/30 mL reduced-sodium soy sauce

1 tablespoon/15 mL dry sherry (optional)

2 teaspoons/10 mL sesame oil (optional)

1½ teaspoons/7.5 mL minced fresh ginger or
 ½ teaspoon/2.5 mL ground ginger

½ teaspoon/2.5 mL black pepper

SOUP

2 cans (14½ ounces/410 grams each) reduced-sodium chicken broth

1 cup/250 mL water

1½ cups/350 mL halved pea pods or 1 package (6 ounces/170 grams) frozen pea pods, thawed, cut in half

1 cup/250 mL thinly sliced carrots

1½ cups/350 mL bean sprouts

¼ cup/60 mL thinly sliced green onions

Heat broiler. Spray rack of broiler pan with nonstick cooking spray or oil lightly.

For meatballs, combine turkey, oats, ¼ cup/60 mL broth, soy sauce, sherry and sesame oil, if desired, ginger and pepper in large bowl; mix lightly but thoroughly. Shape into 1-inch meatballs; place on rack of broiler pan.

Broil 6 to 8 inches from heat 7 to 10 minutes or until cooked through.

For soup, combine meatballs with 2 cans broth and water in 4-quart/4-litre saucepan or Dutch oven; bring to a boil over high heat. Add pea pods and carrots; cook 1 to 2 minutes or until vegetables are crisp-tender. Turn off heat; add bean sprouts and green onions. Serve immediately.

MAKES 6 SERVINGS

GARDEN TURKEY BURGERS

1 cup/250 mL shredded cabbage

¼ cup/60 mL shredded carrots

1 tablespoon/15 mL minced parsley

1 cup/250 mL fat-free plain yogurt, divided

1 teaspoon/5 mL grainy Dijon-style mustard

1 pound/454 grams ground turkey breast or extra lean ground beef

¾ cup/175 mL **Quaker® 100% Whole Grain Large Flake Oats** or **Quaker® 100% Whole Grain Quick Oats** (uncooked)

¼ cup/60 mL finely chopped onion

1 large clove garlic, minced

½ teaspoon/2.5 mL salt

¼ teaspoon/1.25 mL black pepper

4 whole wheat sandwich rolls

1 cup/250 mL packed spinach leaves

4 tomato slices

Combine cabbage, carrots, parsley, ½ cup/125 mL yogurt and mustard in medium bowl; mix well. Cover and chill.

Combine turkey, oats, remaining ½ cup/125 mL yogurt, onion, garlic, salt and pepper in large bowl; mix lightly but thoroughly. Shape mixture into four ½-inch-thick patties.

Broil about 4 inches from heat 3 to 4 minutes on each side or until instant-read thermometer registers 170°F/77°C (160°F/71°C for beef).

To serve, place spinach on roll bottom; top with burger, tomato slice, cabbage mixture and roll top.

MAKES 4 SERVINGS

MEATLOAF
FOCACCIA
SANDWICH

SPREAD

- 1 ounce/30 grams sun-dried tomatoes (not in oil)
- ½ cup/125 mL fat-free or reduced-fat mayonnaise
- 1 clove garlic, minced

  Dash hot pepper sauce

MEATLOAF

- 1½ pounds/680 grams lean ground beef or ground turkey breast
- ¾ cup/175 mL **Quaker® 100% Whole Grain Large Flake Oats or Quaker® 100% Whole Grain Quick Oats** (uncooked)
- ½ cup/125 mL thinly sliced green onions
- ½ cup/125 mL fat-free (skim) milk
- 1 egg, lightly beaten
- 1 teaspoon/5 mL dried thyme leaves
- 1 teaspoon/5 mL salt
- ½ teaspoon/2.5 mL black pepper

SANDWICH FIXINGS

- 1 loaf focaccia bread, about 8×10 inches (about 1½ pounds/680 grams)
- 8 slices reduced-fat Swiss or part-skim mozzarella cheese
- 8 large lettuce leaves

Heat oven to 350°F/180°C. For spread, soften tomatoes according to package directions; coarsely chop. Combine tomatoes, mayonnaise, garlic and hot pepper sauce in small bowl; mix well. Cover and chill.

For meatloaf, combine beef, oats, green onions, milk, egg, thyme, salt and pepper in large bowl; mix lightly but thoroughly. Press mixture evenly into 9×5-inch metal loaf pan.

Bake 60 to 75 minutes to medium doneness or until thermometer inserted into centre of meatloaf registers 160°F/71°C for beef (170°F/77°C for turkey) and juices show no pink colour. Drain any juices. Let stand 5 minutes before slicing.

Cut focaccia into eight rectangles; cut each rectangle in half horizontally. Spread 1 tablespoon/15 mL spread on inside surfaces of each focaccia piece. Cut meatloaf into eight slices; place on half of focaccia rectangles. Top with cheese and lettuce; cover with remaining pieces of focaccia. Serve warm.

MAKES 8 SERVINGS

GARDEN-FRESH
TURKEY BURGERS

1   pound/454 grams 99% lean ground turkey breast

1   cup/250 mL **Quaker® 100% Whole Grain Large Flake Oats** or **Quaker® 100% Whole Grain Quick Oats** (uncooked)

¾   cup/175 mL finely chopped onion

¾   cup/175 mL finely chopped red or green bell pepper

½   cup/125 mL shredded zucchini (about 1 small)

¼   cup/60 mL ketchup

2   cloves garlic, minced

½   teaspoon/2.5 mL salt (optional)

6   whole wheat hamburger buns, split, toasted

½   cup/125 mL fat-free sour cream

      Lettuce and tomato slices (optional)

Spray rack of broiler pan lightly with nonstick cooking spray.

Combine turkey, oats, onion, bell pepper, zucchini, ketchup, garlic and, if desired, salt in medium bowl, mixing lightly but thoroughly. Shape into six ½-inch-thick patties.

Broil or grill patties 7 to 9 minutes on each side or until golden brown and no longer pink in centre.

Serve on buns with rounded tablespoon/15 mL sour cream per serving. Garnish with lettuce and tomato, if desired.

MAKES 6 SERVINGS

VARIATION: If 99% lean ground turkey breast is not available, other ground turkey may be substituted. Proceed as recipe directs.

MEDITERRANEAN DEVILLED CHICKEN SALAD

DRESSING

- ¼ cup/60 mL frozen apple juice concentrate, thawed
- 2 tablespoons/30 mL white wine vinegar
- 2 teaspoons/10 mL coarse Dijon mustard
- ¾ teaspoon/3.75 mL ground cumin
- ⅛ teaspoon/0.625 mL ground red pepper

SALAD

- 4 cups/1 litre torn salad greens
- 2 medium oranges, peeled and sectioned
- 1 red bell pepper, cut into strips
- ½ cup/125 mL sliced red onion
- ¼ cup/60 mL chopped cilantro or parsley

CHICKEN

- ¾ cup/175 mL **Quaker® 100% Whole Grain Large Flake Oats or Quaker® 100% Whole Grain Quick Oats** (uncooked)
- ¼ cup/60 mL grated Parmesan cheese
- ½ teaspoon/2.5 mL ground cumin
- 4 boneless skinless chicken breasts (about 1 pound/454 grams)
- 2 tablespoons/30 mL coarse Dijon mustard

For dressing, combine juice concentrate, vinegar, 2 teaspoons/10 mL mustard, ¾ teaspoon/3.75 mL cumin and red pepper in small bowl. Mix until thoroughly blended; chill.

For salad, combine greens, oranges, bell pepper, red onion and cilantro in large shallow bowl or platter; cover and chill.

Heat broiler. Lightly spray rack of broiler pan with nonstick cooking spray.

Place oats, Parmesan cheese and ½ teaspoon/2.5 mL cumin in blender container or food processor bowl; cover. Blend on high speed or process about 1 minute, stopping occasionally to stir. Set aside.

Pound each chicken breast between sheets of waxed paper to ¼-inch thickness. Spread 2 tablespoons/30 mL mustard thinly over both sides of chicken; coat with oat mixture. Place on broiler pan; spray one side evenly with nonstick cooking spray to coat completely, about 10 seconds.

Broil about 6 inches from heat 3 to 4 minutes; remove pan from broiler. Turn over; spray with nonstick cooking spray to coat, about 10 seconds. Broil additional 3 to 4 minutes or until golden brown and no longer pink in centre.

Toss salad with dressing; place warm chicken on top. Serve with additional orange wedges and cilantro, if desired.

MAKES 4 SERVINGS

HEARTY ENTRÉES AND SIDES

TACO LOAF

MEATLOAF

1½ pounds/680 grams 80% lean ground beef

¾ cup/175 mL **Quaker® 100% Whole Grain Large Flake Oats** or **Quaker® 100% Whole Grain Quick Oats** (uncooked)

½ cup/125 mL thick and chunky salsa

1 egg, lightly beaten

1 packet (1 to 1.25 ounces/30 to 35 grams) reduced-sodium taco seasoning mix

TOPPINGS

¾ cup/175 mL thick and chunky salsa

½ cup/125 mL (2 ounces/60 grams) shredded reduced-fat Cheddar cheese

1½ cups/350 mL shredded lettuce

½ cup/125 mL chopped tomato

½ cup/125 mL sliced ripe olives

Reduced-fat sour cream (optional)

Heat oven to 350°F/180°C. Combine beef, oats, ½ cup/125 mL salsa, egg and seasoning mix in large bowl; mix lightly but thoroughly. Press mixture evenly into 8- or 9-inch square metal baking pan.

Bake 40 to 45 minutes to medium doneness or until thermometer inserted into centre of meatloaf registers 160°F/71°C and juices show no pink colour. Drain any juices.

Top with ¾ cup/175 mL salsa and sprinkle with Cheddar cheese. Bake 5 minutes or until cheese has melted. Let stand 5 minutes before slicing.

Cut meatloaf into six squares to serve. Top with lettuce, tomato, olives and sour cream, if desired.

MAKES 6 SERVINGS

TRADITIONAL STUFFING

2 tablespoons/30 mL olive oil

2 cups/500 mL sliced celery

1 cup/250 mL chopped onion

1½ tablespoons/22.5 mL poultry seasoning

1 teaspoon/5 mL sage

½ teaspoon/2.5 mL salt

¼ teaspoon/1.25 mL black pepper

8 cups/2 litres fresh bread cubes (white, whole wheat or multi-grain)

2 cups/500 mL **Quaker® 100% Whole Grain Large Flake Oats** or **Quaker® 100% Whole Grain Quick Oats** (uncooked)

1 cup/250 mL chopped apple

1 cup/250 mL dried cranberries

¼ cup/60 mL chopped parsley

½ cup/125 mL chopped walnuts

1 can (10¾ ounces/305 grams) chicken broth

This is enough stuffing for a 13- to 19-pound/6- to -8.6-kg turkey. If using a larger turkey, double the recipe and bake any remaining stuffing in a casserole dish for about 1 hour or until warmed through.

Heat oil in large saucepan over medium-low heat. Add celery, onion, poultry seasoning, sage, salt and pepper; cook 4 to 5 minutes or until tender. Remove from heat.

Combine bread cubes, oats, apple, cranberries, parsley and walnuts in large bowl; mix well. Add onion mixture and chicken broth. Mix until bread is evenly coated.

Stuff into body and neck of turkey. Immediately after stuffing, place turkey in oven and begin roasting.

MAKES 9 CUPS/2.25 LITRES

CUBAN MEATBALL KABOBS

SALSA

- 1 cup/250 mL mild or medium chunky salsa
- 1 cup/250 mL peeled, diced ripe mango or peaches
- 2 tablespoons/30 mL coarsely chopped cilantro

MEATBALLS

- 1 pound/454 grams lean ground beef
- ¾ cup/175 mL **Quaker® 100% Whole Grain Large Flake Oats** or **Quaker® 100% Whole Grain Quick Oats** (uncooked)
- ¾ cup/175 mL finely chopped red onion
- ¼ cup/60 mL fat-free (skim) milk
- 1 clove garlic, minced
- 1½ tablespoons/22.5 mL coarsely chopped fresh cilantro
- 1 teaspoon/5 mL dried oregano leaves
- ¾ teaspoon/3.75 mL salt (optional)
- ½ teaspoon/2.5 mL ground cumin
- 6 (6-inch) flour or corn tortillas, warmed

tip

To warm tortillas, stack between microwave-safe paper towels. Microwave on HIGH 15 to 30 seconds or until warm.

For salsa, combine all ingredients in medium bowl; mix well. Set aside.

For meatballs, combine ground beef, oats, onion, milk, garlic, cilantro, oregano, salt, if desired, and cumin in large bowl, mixing lightly but thoroughly. Shape into eighteen 1½-inch meatballs; arrange on six metal skewers.

Broil 4 to 5 inches from heat source 5 to 8 minutes on each side or until beef is not pink in centre and juices show no pink colour.

Remove meatballs from skewers; serve with salsa and tortillas.

MAKES 6 SERVINGS

GARDEN SALMON LOAF

SAUCE

¾ cup/175 mL frozen peas, thawed

¾ cup/175 mL low fat plain yogurt

1 tablespoon/15 mL Dijon-style mustard

1 tablespoon/15 mL chopped fresh dill weed or 1 teaspoon/5 mL dried dill

Black pepper, to taste

SALMON LOAF

2 cans (15½ ounces/440 grams each) salmon, drained, skin and bones removed

1 cup/250 mL shredded carrots

1 cup/250 mL **Quaker® 100% Whole Grain Large Flake Oats** or **Quaker® 100% Whole Grain Quick Oats** (uncooked)

1 cup/250 mL low fat plain yogurt

¾ cup/175 mL sliced green onions

1 can (2½ ounces/70 grams) sliced ripe olives (optional)

3 egg whites, lightly beaten

⅓ cup/75 mL chopped green bell pepper

1 tablespoon/15 mL Dijon-style mustard

¼ teaspoon/1.25 mL black pepper

For sauce, combine peas, ¾ cup/175 mL yogurt, 1 tablespoon/15 mL mustard, dill and black pepper, to taste, in small bowl; mix well. Cover and chill.

Heat oven to 350°F/180°C. Spray 8×4-inch or 9×5-inch loaf pan with nonstick cooking spray.

Combine salmon, carrots, oats, 1 cup/250 mL yogurt, green onions, olives, if desired, egg whites, bell pepper, 1 tablespoon/15 mL mustard and ¼ teaspoon/1.25 mL black pepper in large bowl; mix lightly but thoroughly. Press into prepared pan. Bake 50 to 60 minutes or until light golden brown. Let stand 5 minutes before slicing. Serve immediately with sauce.

MAKES 10 SERVINGS

SPICY OAT-CRUSTED CHICKEN WITH SUNSHINE SALSA

SALSA

¾ cup/175 mL prepared salsa

¾ cup/175 mL coarsely chopped orange sections

CHICKEN

2 tablespoons/30 mL canola oil

1 tablespoon/15 mL margarine, melted

2 teaspoons/10 mL chili powder

1 teaspoon/5 mL garlic powder

1 teaspoon/5 mL ground cumin

¾ teaspoon/3.75 mL salt

1½ cups/350 mL **Quaker® 100% Whole Grain Quick Oats** (uncooked)

1 egg, lightly beaten

1 tablespoon/15 mL water

4 boneless skinless chicken breasts (about 5 to 6 ounces/140 to 170 grams each)

Chopped fresh cilantro (optional)

For salsa, combine ingredients in small bowl. Cover and chill.

Heat oven to 375°F/190°C. Line baking sheet with aluminum foil. Stir together oil, margarine, chili powder, garlic powder, cumin and salt in flat, shallow dish. Add oats, stirring until evenly moistened.

Beat egg and water with fork until frothy in second flat, shallow dish. Dip chicken into egg mixture, then coat completely in seasoned oats. Place chicken on foil-lined baking sheet. Pat any extra oat mixture onto chicken.

Bake 30 minutes or until chicken is cooked through and oat coating is golden brown. Serve with salsa. Garnish with cilantro, if desired.

MAKES 4 SERVINGS

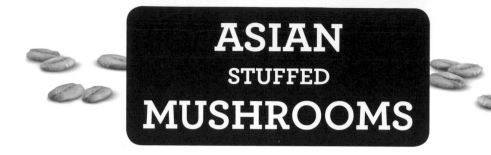

ASIAN STUFFED MUSHROOMS

24 large mushrooms (about 2 pounds/910 grams)

½ cup/125 mL reduced-sodium soy sauce

¼ cup/60 mL dry sherry

½ pound/227 grams ground turkey

¾ cup/175 mL **Quaker® 100% Whole Grain Large Flake Oats** or **Quaker® 100% Whole Grain Quick Oats** (uncooked)

½ cup/125 mL sliced green onions

¼ cup/60 mL finely chopped red or green bell pepper

1 egg white, lightly beaten

1 tablespoon/15 mL Dijon-style mustard

2 cloves garlic, minced

Remove stems from mushrooms; reserve stems. Place mushroom caps in large bowl. Combine soy sauce and sherry in small bowl; pour over mushrooms. Cover and marinate at least 1 hour, stirring once after 30 minutes.

Chop reserved mushroom stems finely. Place in large bowl with turkey, oats, green onions, bell pepper, egg white, mustard and garlic; mix well.

Drain mushroom caps, reserving marinade. Fill caps with turkey mixture, packing well and mounding slightly. Place on broiler pan. Brush tops with reserved marinade.

Broil 7 to 8 inches from heat 15 to 18 minutes or until turkey is cooked through. Serve immediately.

MAKES 24 APPETIZERS

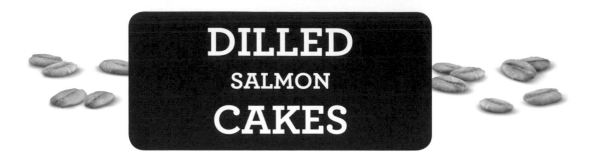

DILLED SALMON CAKES

SAUCE

- ½ cup/125 mL fat-free plain yogurt
- ⅓ cup/75 mL seeded chopped tomato
- ⅓ cup/75 mL seeded chopped cucumber
- 1 tablespoon/15 mL finely chopped onion
- 1 tablespoon/15 mL finely chopped fresh dill or 1 teaspoon/5 mL dried dill weed

SALMON CAKES

- 1 can (14¾ ounces/418 grams) pink salmon, drained, skin and bones removed
- ¾ cup/175 mL **Quaker® 100% Whole Grain Large Flake Oats** or **Quaker® 100% Whole Grain Quick Oats** (uncooked)
- ⅓ cup/75 mL fat-free (skim) milk
- ¼ cup/60 mL liquid egg substitute with yolk or 1 egg, lightly beaten
- 2 tablespoons/30 mL finely chopped onion
- 1 tablespoon/15 mL finely chopped fresh dill or 1 teaspoon/5 mL dried dill weed
- ¼ teaspoon/1.25 mL salt (optional)

For sauce, combine yogurt, tomato, cucumber, 1 tablespoon/15 mL onion and 1 tablespoon/15 mL dill in small bowl; mix well. Cover and chill.

Combine salmon, oats, milk, egg substitute, 2 tablespoons/30 mL onion, 1 tablespoon/15 mL dill and, if desired, salt in medium bowl; mix well. Let stand 5 minutes. Shape into six oval patties.

Spray large nonstick skillet lightly with nonstick cooking spray. Cook salmon cakes over medium heat 3 to 4 minutes on each side or until golden brown and heated through. Serve with sauce.

MAKES 6 SERVINGS

BROCCOLI-STUFFED
TOMATOES

4   large tomatoes (about
    1 pound/454 grams)

1   package (10 ounces/
    285 grams) frozen
    chopped broccoli, thawed
    and well drained

⅔   cup/150 mL **Quaker®
    100% Whole Grain Large
    Flake Oats** (uncooked)

½   cup/125 mL low fat small-curd
    cottage cheese

¼   cup/60 mL chopped onion

1½ teaspoons/7.5 mL minced fresh
    basil or ½ teaspoon/2.5 mL
    dried basil leaves

1   clove garlic, minced

¼   cup/60 mL finely shredded
    Parmesan or Swiss cheese

Heat oven to 350°F/180°C.

Slice ¼ inch from stem end of
each tomato. Scoop out pulp and
seeds; discard or reserve for another
use. Arrange tomatoes in shallow
1-quart/1-litre glass baking dish.

Combine broccoli, oats, cottage
cheese, onion, basil and garlic in
medium bowl; mix well. Fill tomatoes
with mixture; sprinkle with Parmesan
cheese.

Bake 20 to 25 minutes or until
heated through.

MAKES 4 SERVINGS

HEARTY
MEATBALL
STEW

1 pound/454 grams ground turkey breast or extra lean ground beef

¾ cup/175 mL **Quaker® 100% Whole Grain Large Flake Oats or Quaker® 100% Whole Grain Quick Oats** (uncooked)

1 can (8 ounces/225 grams) no-salt-added tomato sauce, divided

1½ teaspoons/7.5 mL garlic powder

1½ teaspoons/7.5 mL dried thyme leaves, divided

2 cans (14½ ounces/410 grams each) 70% less sodium, fat-free chicken broth

¾ teaspoon/3.75 mL salt (optional)

2½ cups/600 mL any frozen vegetable blend (do not thaw)

⅓ cup/75 mL ditalini or other small pasta

¼ cup/60 mL water

2 tablespoons/30 mL cornstarch

Heat broiler. Lightly spray rack of broiler pan with nonstick cooking spray.

Combine turkey, oats, ⅓ cup/75 mL tomato sauce, garlic powder and 1 teaspoon/5 mL thyme in large bowl; mix lightly but thoroughly. Transfer to sheet of aluminum foil or waxed paper. Pat mixture into 9×6-inch rectangle. Cut into 1½-inch squares; roll each square into a ball. Arrange meatballs on broiler pan.

Broil 6 to 8 inches from heat about 6 minutes or until cooked through, turning once.

Bring broth, remaining tomato sauce, remaining ½ teaspoon/2.5 mL thyme and, if desired, salt to a boil in 4-quart/4-litre saucepan or Dutch oven over medium-high heat. Add vegetables and pasta; return to a boil. Reduce heat, cover and simmer 10 minutes or until vegetables and pasta are tender.

Stir together water and cornstarch in small bowl until smooth. Add to broth along with meatballs. Cook and stir until broth is thickened. Spoon into bowls.

MAKES 6 SERVINGS

PRIZE-WINNING
MEATLOAF

1½ pounds/680 grams 90% lean ground beef

1 cup/250 mL tomato juice or tomato sauce

¾ cup/175 mL **Quaker® 100% Whole Grain Large Flake Oats** or **Quaker® 100% Whole Grain Quick Oats** (uncooked)

1 egg or 2 egg whites, lightly beaten

¼ cup/60 mL chopped onion

½ teaspoon/2.5 mL salt (optional)

¼ teaspoon/1.25 mL black pepper

Heat oven to 350°F/180°C.

Combine beef, tomato juice, oats, egg, onion, salt, if desired, and pepper in large bowl, mixing lightly but thoroughly. Shape into 8×4-inch loaf on rack in broiler pan.

Bake 1 hour to medium (160°F/71°C) doneness, until no longer pink in centre and juices show no pink colour. Let stand 5 minutes.

MAKES 8 SERVINGS

VARIATIONS:

- Customize meatloaf by adding one of the following: ½ cup/125 mL frozen (thawed) or canned (drained) corn; ½ cup/125 mL chopped green or red bell pepper; 1 jar (2½ ounces/70 grams) sliced mushrooms, drained; ⅓ cup/75 mL grated Parmesan cheese; or 2 tablespoons/30 mL finely chopped fresh parsley or cilantro.
- Sprinkle top of baked meatloaf with 1 cup/250 mL shredded cheese. Return to oven for 3 minutes to melt cheese.
- Spoon heated prepared spaghetti sauce, pizza sauce, barbecue sauce or salsa over each serving.

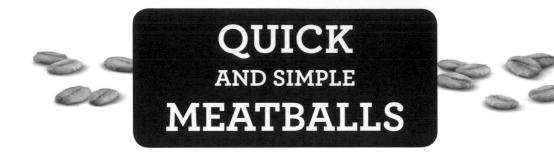

QUICK
AND SIMPLE
MEATBALLS

1½ pounds/680 grams ground beef

¾ cup/175 mL **Quaker® 100% Whole Grain Large Flake Oats** or **Quaker® 100% Whole Grain Quick Oats** (uncooked)

½ cup/125 mL chopped onion or green bell pepper

½ cup/125 mL tomato sauce or ketchup

1 egg

½ teaspoon/2.5 mL salt (optional)

¼ teaspoon/1.25 mL black pepper

Sweet and Sour Glaze or Sherried Mushroom Glaze (recipes follow)

Heat oven to 400°F/200°C. Combine all ingredients; mix well. Shape into 1-inch balls. Place on rack in shallow baking pan.

Bake 18 to 20 minutes or until medium doneness (160°F/71°C). Serve immediately with Sweet and Sour Glaze, Sherried Mushroom Glaze or your own favorite sauce.

MAKES 48 MEATBALLS

SWEET AND SOUR GLAZE: Combine 1 cup/250 mL chili sauce or ketchup and ½ cup/125 mL grape jelly in small saucepan. Heat through, stirring occasionally. Serve warm with meatballs.

SHERRIED MUSHROOM GLAZE: Combine 1 can (10¾ ounces/305 grams) cream of mushroom soup, 2 tablespoons/30 mL sherry and 2 tablespoons/30 mL milk in small saucepan. (If desired, omit sherry and use ¼ cup/60 mL milk.) Heat through, stirring occasionally. Serve warm with meatballs.

THREE PEPPER OAT PILAF

1 tablespoon/15 mL olive oil

½ cup/125 mL chopped red bell pepper

½ cup/125 mL chopped yellow bell pepper

½ cup/125 mL chopped mushrooms

½ cup/125 mL sliced green onions

2 cloves garlic, minced

1¾ cups/450 mL **Quaker® 100% Whole Grain Large Flake Oats** (uncooked)

2 egg whites or 1 egg, lightly beaten

¾ cup/175 mL low fat chicken broth

2 tablespoons/30 mL minced fresh basil or 2 teaspoons/10 mL dried basil leaves

½ teaspoon/2.5 mL salt

¼ teaspoon/1.25 mL black pepper

Heat oil in 10-inch nonstick skillet over medium heat. Add bell peppers, mushrooms, green onions and garlic; cook, stirring occasionally, until vegetables are crisp-tender, about 2 minutes.

Mix oats and egg whites in large bowl until oats are evenly coated. Add oats to vegetable mixture in skillet. Cook over medium heat, stirring occasionally, until oats are dry and separated, about 5 to 6 minutes.

Add broth, basil, salt and black pepper. Continue cooking, stirring occasionally, 2 to 3 minutes or until liquid is absorbed. Serve immediately.

MAKES 6 SERVINGS

GARDEN PIZZAS

CRUST

⅔ cup/150 mL warm water (105°F to 115°F/40°C to 46°C)

2¼ teaspoons/11.25 mL quick-rising yeast

1 tablespoon/15 mL olive oil

2 teaspoons/10 mL granulated sugar

1⅓ cups/325 mL all-purpose flour

¾ cup/175 mL **Quaker® 100% Whole Grain Large Flake Oats or Quaker® 100% Whole Grain Quick Oats** (uncooked)

TOPPINGS

¼ cup/60 mL shredded or grated Parmesan cheese

1½ cups/350 mL (6 ounces/170 grams) shredded part-skim mozzarella cheese, divided

½ cup/125 mL thinly sliced green bell pepper

½ cup/125 mL thinly sliced red onion

¼ cup/60 mL chopped fresh basil or 4 teaspoons/20 mL dried basil leaves

2 cloves garlic, minced

4 plum tomatoes, thinly sliced (about 2 cups/500 mL)

Heat oven to 425°F/220°C. Spray cookie sheets with nonstick cooking spray or oil lightly.

Combine water, yeast, oil and sugar in small bowl; mix well. Let stand 10 minutes or until foamy.

Combine flour and oats in large bowl. Add yeast mixture; blend with electric mixer at low speed until dry ingredients are moistened. Increase speed to medium; beat 2 minutes.

Turn dough out onto lightly floured surface. Knead 1 minute. Shape dough into ball; place in greased bowl, turning once to coat. Cover; let rise in warm place 20 minutes or until nearly doubled in size.

Punch dough down; divide into four portions. On cookie sheets, pat each portion of dough into 6-inch circle. Top with Parmesan cheese, ¾ cup/175 mL mozzarella cheese, bell pepper, red onion, basil, garlic and tomatoes, in that order, dividing evenly. Sprinkle with remaining ¾ cup/175 mL mozzarella cheese.

Bake 20 minutes or until crust is golden brown.

MAKES 4 PIZZAS

 **tip**

Pizzas may be grilled. After shaping crusts, grill over medium-hot coals 2 to 4 minutes or until bottoms are golden brown. Remove from grill. On browned side of crusts, layer toppings as directed. Return to grill. Cover; grill 4 to 6 minutes or until bottoms are golden brown and cheese begins to melt.

SAUCY STUFFED PEPPERS

6 medium green bell peppers

1¼ cups/300 mL water

2 cups/500 mL low-sodium tomato juice, divided

1 can (6 ounces/170 grams) tomato paste

1 teaspoon/5 mL dried oregano leaves, divided

½ teaspoon/2.5 mL dried basil leaves

½ teaspoon/2.5 mL garlic powder, divided

1 pound/454 grams lean ground beef

1½ cups/350 mL **Quaker® 100% Whole Grain Large Flake Oats or Quaker® 100% Whole Grain Quick Oats** (uncooked)

1 medium tomato, chopped

¼ cup/60 mL chopped carrot

¼ cup/60 mL chopped onion

Heat oven to 350°F/180°C. Cut bell peppers lengthwise in half; remove membranes and seeds. Set aside.

For sauce, combine water, 1 cup/250 mL tomato juice, tomato paste, ½ teaspoon/2.5 mL oregano, basil and ¼ teaspoon/1.25 mL garlic powder in medium saucepan over medium heat. Simmer 10 to 15 minutes. Set aside.

For filling, combine beef, oats, tomato, carrot and onion with remaining 1 cup/250 mL tomato juice, remaining ½ teaspoon/2.5 mL oregano and ¼ teaspoon/1.25 mL garlic powder in large bowl, mixing lightly but thoroughly.

Fill each bell pepper half with about ⅓ cup/75 mL meat mixture. Place in 13×9-inch glass baking dish; pour reserved sauce evenly over bell peppers.

Bake 45 to 50 minutes to medium doneness or until thermometer inserted into centre of meat registers 160°F/71°C and juices show no pink colour.

MAKES 12 SERVINGS

BBQ MEATLOAF

BBQ SAUCE

¼ cup/60 mL ketchup

2 tablespoons/30 mL firmly packed brown sugar

1 teaspoon/5 mL dry mustard

MEATLOAF

⅔ cup/150 mL fat-free (skim) milk

3 large egg whites, slightly beaten

½ cup/125 mL finely chopped celery

½ cup/125 mL chopped onion

¼ cup/60 mL snipped fresh parsley or 1½ teaspoons/7.5 mL parsley flakes

½ teaspoon/2.5 mL sage

¼ teaspoon/1.25 mL salt (optional)

¼ teaspoon/1.25 mL black pepper

1 pound/454 grams extra lean ground beef

1 cup/250 mL **Quaker® Oat Bran** hot cereal (uncooked)

Heat oven to 350°F/180°C. For sauce, combine all ingredients in small bowl; mix well. Set aside.

For meatloaf, combine milk, egg whites, celery, onion, parsley, sage, salt, if desired, and pepper in large bowl; mix well. Add ground beef and oat bran; mix lightly but thoroughly. Press into 8×4-inch loaf pan.

Bake 50 minutes. Remove meatloaf from oven; spoon BBQ sauce over top. Bake additional 10 minutes. Let stand 5 minutes before slicing.

MAKES 6 SERVINGS

tip

Substitute purchased barbecue sauce instead of making BBQ sauce.

GARDEN-STYLE
TURKEY LOAF

1½ pounds/680 grams lean ground turkey breast

1 package (10 ounces/285 grams) frozen chopped spinach, thawed and drained

1 cup/250 mL **Quaker® 100% Whole Grain Large Flake Oats or Quaker® 100% Whole Grain Quick Oats** (uncooked)

½ cup/125 mL finely chopped onion

½ cup/125 mL shredded carrots

2 egg whites or 1 egg, lightly beaten

⅓ cup/75 mL fat-free (skim) milk

1½ teaspoons/7.5 mL Italian seasoning blend

1 teaspoon/5 mL salt (optional)

¼ teaspoon/1.25 mL black pepper

Heat oven to 350°F/180°C.

Combine all ingredients in large bowl, mixing lightly but thoroughly. Shape mixture into 9×5-inch loaf in 13×9-inch baking pan or on rack of broiler pan.

Bake 1 hour or until thermometer registers 170°F/77°C and centre is no longer pink. Let stand 5 minutes before slicing.

MAKES 8 SERVINGS

VARIATIONS: Lean ground beef may be substituted for ground turkey breast. Proceed with recipe. Bake 50 to 55 minutes to medium (160°F/71°C) doneness, until not pink in centre and juices show no pink colour. One-half cup/125 mL finely chopped green or red bell pepper may be substituted for spinach.

MINI TEX-MEX MEATLOAVES

MEATLOAVES

1½ pounds/680 grams lean ground beef

¾ cup/175 mL **Quaker® 100% Whole Grain Large Flake Oats** or **Quaker® 100% Whole Grain Quick Oats** (uncooked)

½ cup/125 mL mild chunky salsa

¼ cup/60 mL chopped cilantro

1 egg, lightly beaten

2 teaspoons/10 mL chili powder

1½ teaspoons/7.5 mL ground cumin

½ teaspoon/2.5 mL salt (optional)

TOPPING

¾ cup/175 mL mild chunky salsa

¾ cup/175 mL (3 ounces/90 grams) shredded Cheddar cheese

Heat oven to 400°F/200°C.

For meatloaves, combine ground beef, oats, ½ cup/125 mL salsa, cilantro, egg, chili powder, cumin and, if desired, salt in large bowl, mixing lightly but thoroughly. Press approximately ⅓ cup/75 mL beef mixture into each of 12 medium muffin pan cups.

Bake 15 to 20 minutes to medium (160°F/71°C) doneness, until not pink in centre and juices show no pink colour. Remove meatloaves from oven.

Top each meatloaf with 1 tablespoon/15 mL salsa and 1 tablespoon/15 mL Cheddar cheese. Return to oven; continue baking 3 minutes or until cheese is melted. Use narrow metal spatula or knife to loosen and then lift meatloaves from pan.

MAKES 12 MINI MEATLOAVES

SPINACH-STUFFED
TURKEY MEATLOAF

- 1 cup/250 mL coarsely chopped mushrooms
- ¼ cup/60 mL chopped onion
- 1 package (10 ounces/285 grams) frozen chopped spinach, thawed and drained
- ½ cup/125 mL (2 ounces/60 grams) shredded part-skim mozzarella cheese, divided
- ¼ cup/60 mL grated Parmesan cheese
- 1 pound/454 grams 99% lean ground turkey breast
- ¾ cup/175 mL **Quaker® 100% Whole Grain Large Flake Oats or Quaker® 100% Whole Grain Quick Oats** (uncooked)
- ½ cup/125 mL fat-free (skim) milk
- 1 egg white, lightly beaten
- 1 teaspoon/5 mL Italian seasoning blend
- ½ teaspoon/2.5 mL salt (optional)
- ¼ teaspoon/1.25 mL black pepper

tip

If ground turkey breast is not available, 1 pound/454 grams 90% lean ground turkey may be substituted. Proceed as recipe directs.

Heat oven to 375°F/190°C. Lightly spray medium skillet with nonstick cooking spray.

Cook mushrooms and onion over medium-low heat 4 minutes or until onion is tender; remove from heat. Add spinach, ¼ cup/60 mL mozzarella cheese and Parmesan cheese; mix well. Set aside.

Combine turkey, oats, milk, egg white, Italian seasoning, salt, if desired, and pepper in large bowl; mix lightly but thoroughly. Spoon ⅔ of mixture lengthwise down centre of 11X7-inch glass baking dish. Form deep indentation down middle; fill indentation with reserved spinach mixture. Top with remaining turkey mixture, forming loaf. Seal edges to completely enclose spinach filling.

Bake 30 to 35 minutes or until thermometer inserted into centre of meatloaf registers 170°F/77°C and juices show no pink colour. Remove from oven; sprinkle with remaining ¼ cup/60 mL mozzarella cheese. Return to oven 1 to 2 minutes or until cheese melts. Let stand 5 minutes before slicing.

MAKES 8 SERVINGS

IN THE BREAD BASKET

CINNAMON OAT ROLLS

1   pound/454 grams frozen bread dough, thawed according to package directions

1   cup/250 mL **Quaker® 100% Whole Grain Large Flake Oats** or **Quaker® 100% Whole Grain Quick Oats** (uncooked)

⅓   cup/75 mL firmly packed brown sugar

2   teaspoons/10 mL ground cinnamon

⅓   cup/75 mL (⅔ stick) margarine or butter, melted

¾   cup/175 mL raisins or dried cranberries

¼   cup/60 mL orange marmalade

Let dough stand, covered, at room temperature 15 minutes to relax. Spray 8- or 9-inch square baking pan with nonstick cooking spray.

Combine oats, brown sugar and cinnamon in medium bowl. Add margarine; mix well. Stir in raisins. Set aside.

Roll dough into 12×10-inch rectangle. (Dough will be very elastic.) Spread evenly with oat mixture to within ½ inch of edges. Starting from long side, roll up; pinch seam to seal. With sharp knife, cut into nine slices about 1¼ inches wide; place in prepared pan, cut sides down. Cover loosely with plastic wrap; let rise in warm place 30 minutes or until nearly doubled in size.

Heat oven to 350°F/180°C. Bake 30 to 35 minutes or until golden brown. Cool 5 minutes in pan on wire rack; remove from pan. Spread tops of rolls with marmalade. Serve warm.

MAKES 9 ROLLS

BABY BEAR
BREADS WITH HONEY
BUTTER

3 teaspoons/15 mL quick-rising yeast

2 cups/500 mL bread flour

1½ cups/350 mL whole wheat flour

1 cup/250 mL **Quaker® 100% Whole Grain Large Flake Oats or Quaker® 100% Whole Grain Quick Oats** (uncooked)

⅓ cup/75 mL sunflower seed kernels (optional)

⅓ cup/75 mL firmly packed brown sugar

1½ teaspoons/7.5 mL ground cinnamon

1 teaspoon/5 mL salt

1½ cups/350 mL low fat (2%) milk

1 egg, lightly beaten

5 tablespoons/75 mL stick butter or margarine, melted

Assorted raisins and other chopped dried fruits

Honey Butter (recipe follows)

Bring all ingredients to room temperature by letting them stand on the counter about 30 minutes.

Place yeast in bread machine according to directions in manual. Combine bread flour, whole wheat flour, oats, sunflower seeds, if desired, brown sugar, cinnamon and salt in medium bowl. Combine milk, egg and butter in separate bowl.

Place dry and liquid ingredients in bread machine according to manual. Use machine's dough setting to mix and knead. (Bread will not bake in machine.)

Grease two cookie sheets lightly. Turn dough out of bread machine onto lightly floured surface. Knead 6 to 8 times.

To make bears, roll pieces of dough into four 2½-inch balls for bodies, four 1½-inch balls for heads, sixteen 1-inch balls for hands and feet and eight ¾-inch balls for ears. On cookie sheets, gently place balls together to form two bears on each sheet. Use raisins to make eyes, nose and other decorations. Cover; let rise in warm place 15 to 20 minutes or until nearly doubled in size.

Heat oven to 375°F/190°C. Bake bear breads 12 to 15 minutes or until light golden brown. Carefully remove bears from cookie sheets to wire racks. Cool completely. Store tightly wrapped up to one day. Freeze for longer storage. Serve with Honey Butter.

MAKES 4 BREADS

HONEY BUTTER: Combine ½ cup/125 mL (1 stick) softened butter or margarine and 3 tablespoons/45 mL honey in small bowl; mix until smooth. Store tightly covered in refrigerator.

CONVENTIONAL DIRECTIONS: Combine 1½ cups/350 mL bread flour, whole wheat flour, oats, sunflower seeds, if desired, brown sugar, yeast, cinnamon and salt in large bowl. Heat milk and butter until very warm (120°F to 130°F/49°C to 55°C). Add to flour mixture with egg and blend with electric mixer at low speed until moistened. Beat 3 minutes at medium speed. Stir in enough additional bread flour (about ½ to 1 cup/125 to 250 mL) until soft dough forms and begins to clear sides of bowl. Turn dough out onto lightly floured surface. Knead 5 to 8 minutes or until smooth and elastic. Shape dough into ball; place in greased bowl, turning once. Cover; let rise in warm place 30 minutes or until doubled in size. Punch dough down. Cover; let rest 10 minutes. Shape into bears and bake as directed above.

tip

Refrigerated ingredients (except eggs) can be warmed to room temperature quickly by microwaving them for 15 to 20 seconds on HIGH.

QUAKER'S
BEST OATMEAL
BREAD

5¾ to 6¼ cups/1.45 to 1.56 litres all-purpose flour

2½ cups/600 mL **Quaker® 100% Whole Grain Large Flake Oats** or **Quaker® 100% Whole Grain Quick Oats** (uncooked)

¼ cup/60 mL granulated sugar

4½ teaspoons/22.5 mL quick-rising yeast

2½ teaspoons/12.5 mL salt

1½ cups/350 mL water

1¼ cups/300 mL fat-free (skim) milk

¼ cup/60 mL (½ stick) margarine or butter

Combine 3 cups/750 mL flour, oats, sugar, yeast and salt in large bowl; mix well. Heat water, milk and margarine in small saucepan until very warm (120°F to 130°F/49°C to 55°C). Add to flour mixture. Blend with electric mixer at low speed until moistened; beat 3 minutes at medium speed. By hand, gradually stir in enough remaining flour to make stiff dough.

Turn dough out onto lightly floured surface. Knead 5 to 8 minutes or until smooth and elastic. Shape dough into ball; place in greased bowl, turning once. Cover; let rise in warm place 30 minutes or until doubled in size.

Punch down dough. Cover; let rest 10 minutes. Divide dough in half; shape to form loaves. Place in two greased 8×4-inch or 9×5-inch loaf pans. Cover; let rise in warm place 15 minutes or until nearly doubled in size.

Heat oven to 375°F/190°C. Bake 45 to 50 minutes or until dark golden brown. Remove from pans to wire rack. Cool completely before slicing.

MAKES 2 LOAVES (16 SERVINGS EACH)

tip

If desired, brush tops of loaves lightly with melted margarine or butter and sprinkle with additional oats after placing in pans.

SOFT OATY PRETZELS

3   to 3½ cups/750 to 875 mL all-purpose flour, divided

1½ cups/350 mL **Quaker® 100% Whole Grain Large Flake Oats** or **Quaker® 100% Whole Grain Quick Oats** (uncooked), divided

2   tablespoons/30 mL granulated sugar

2¼ teaspoons/11.25 mL quick-rising yeast

1½ teaspoons/7.5 mL salt

¾   cup/175 mL milk

¾   cup/175 mL water

2   tablespoons/30 mL margarine or butter, softened

1   egg, lightly beaten

Combine 2 cups/500 mL flour, 1¼ cups/300 mL oats, sugar, yeast and salt in large bowl; mix well. Heat milk and water in small saucepan until very warm (120°F to 130°F/49°C to 55°C); stir in margarine. Add to flour mixture. Blend with electric mixer at low speed until moistened; beat 3 minutes at medium speed. By hand, gradually stir in enough remaining flour to make soft dough that pulls away from sides of bowl.

Turn dough out onto lightly floured surface. Knead 5 to 8 minutes or until smooth and elastic, adding additional flour if dough is sticky. Cover loosely with plastic wrap; let dough rest on floured surface 10 minutes.

Heat oven to 350°F/180°C. Lightly grease or spray two large baking sheets with nonstick cooking spray.

Divide dough into 24 equal pieces. Roll each piece into 12-inch-long rope; form into pretzel, letter or number shape. Place on baking sheet. Cover loosely with plastic wrap; let rest 10 minutes or until slightly risen. Brush tops of pretzel with beaten egg; sprinkle with remaining ¼ cup/60 mL oats, pressing lightly.

Bake 15 to 18 minutes or until golden brown. (If baking both sheets at one time, rotate sheets top to bottom and front to back halfway through baking time.) Remove from baking sheets; cool on wire racks. Store tightly covered at room temperature.

MAKES 24 PRETZELS

CARAMEL-
APPLE
FLATBREAD

FLATBREAD

2¼ cups/550 mL all-purpose flour

½ cup/125 mL **Quaker® 100% Whole Grain Large Flake Oats** or
Quaker® 100% Whole Grain Quick Oats (uncooked)

1 tablespoon/15 mL granulated sugar

2¼ teaspoons/11.25 mL quick-rising yeast

½ teaspoon/2.5 mL ground cinnamon

½ teaspoon/2.5 mL salt

¾ cup/175 mL water

1 tablespoon/15 mL vegetable oil

1 egg white

1 cup/250 mL chopped unpeeled apple (about 1 large)

TOPPING

¾ cup/175 mL **Quaker® 100% Whole Grain Large Flake Oats** or
Quaker® 100% Whole Grain Quick Oats (uncooked)

⅔ cup/150 mL firmly packed brown sugar

½ teaspoon/2.5 mL ground cinnamon

¾ cup/175 mL reduced-fat sour cream

¼ cup/60 mL chopped pecans or walnuts

Spray large cookie sheet lightly with nonstick cooking spray.

For bread, combine flour, ½ cup/125 mL oats, granulated sugar, yeast, ½ teaspoon/2.5 mL cinnamon and salt in food processor bowl; pulse machine on and off several times until well mixed.

Heat water and oil in small saucepan until very warm (120°F to 130°F/49°C to 55°C). With motor running, add liquids to flour mixture along with egg white. Process until dough begins to form a ball; continue processing 1 minute.

tip

To prepare flatbread without a food processor, combine 2 cups/ 500 mL flour, oats, granulated sugar, yeast, cinnamon and salt in large bowl. Heat water and oil as directed. Add to flour mixture. Stir, gradually adding enough additional flour as needed to make soft dough that pulls away from sides of bowl. Proceed as directed.

Turn dough out onto lightly floured surface. Knead apples into dough. Pat into 14×11-inch rectangle on cookie sheet. Cover with plastic wrap* and let rise in warm place 40 minutes or until almost doubled in size.

Heat oven to 400°F/200°C.

For topping, combine ¾ cup/175 mL oats, brown sugar, ½ teaspoon/ 2.5 mL cinnamon and sour cream in small bowl; mix well. Spread mixture evenly over top of dough; sprinkle with pecans.

Bake 16 to 18 minutes or until edges are light golden brown. Cool in pan 3 minutes. Remove to wire rack and cool 10 minutes. Cut into squares. Serve warm.

MAKES 16 SERVINGS

To prevent plastic wrap from sticking to dough, spray wrap with nonstick cooking spray first.

ITALIAN
HERBED OATMEAL
FOCACCIA

2 tablespoons/30 mL cornmeal

1½ to 2¼ cups/350 to 550 mL all-purpose flour

1 cup/250 mL **Quaker® 100% Whole Grain Large Flake Oats** or **Quaker® 100% Whole Grain Quick Oats** (uncooked)

2 tablespoons/30 mL Italian seasoning blend, divided

2¼ teaspoons/11.25 mL quick-rising yeast

2 teaspoons/10 mL granulated sugar

1½ teaspoons/7.5 mL garlic salt, divided

1 cup/250 mL water

¼ cup plus 2 tablespoons/90 mL olive oil, divided

4 to 6 sun-dried tomatoes packed in oil, drained and chopped

¼ cup/60 mL shredded Parmesan cheese

Spray 13×9-inch baking pan lightly with nonstick cooking spray; dust with cornmeal.

Combine 1 cup/250 mL flour, oats, 1 tablespoon/15 mL Italian seasoning, yeast, sugar and 1 teaspoon/5 mL garlic salt in large bowl; mix well. Heat water and ¼ cup/60 mL olive oil in small saucepan until very warm (120°F to 130°F/49°C to 55°C). Add to flour mixture; mix well. Gradually stir in enough remaining flour to make soft dough.

Turn dough out onto lightly floured surface. Knead 8 to 10 minutes or until smooth and elastic. Cover; let rest 10 minutes.

Pat dough into prepared pan, pressing dough out to edges of pan. Using fingertips, poke indentations over surface of dough. Brush dough with remaining 2 tablespoons/30 mL oil. Sprinkle with remaining 1 tablespoon/15 mL Italian seasoning and ½ teaspoon/2.5 mL garlic salt. Arrange dried tomatoes across top; sprinkle with cheese. Cover; let rise in warm place 30 minutes or until doubled in size.

Heat oven to 400°F/200°C. Bake 25 to 30 minutes or until golden brown. Cut into squares or strips. Serve warm.

MAKES 12 SERVINGS

OATMEAL HERB BREAD

2½ teaspoons/12.5 mL quick-rising yeast

2¾ cups/675 mL bread flour

1 cup/250 mL **Quaker® 100% Whole Grain Large Flake Oats or Quaker® 100% Whole Grain Quick Oats** (uncooked)

½ cup/125 mL grated Parmesan cheese

1 tablespoon/15 mL granulated sugar

1 teaspoon/5 mL salt

½ teaspoon/2.5 mL Italian seasoning blend or dried dill weed

1⅓ cups/325 mL buttermilk

2 tablespoons/30 mL vegetable oil (preferably olive oil)

Bring all refrigerated ingredients to room temperature by letting them stand on counter about 30 minutes.

Place yeast in bread machine pan according to directions in manual.

Combine flour, oats, Parmesan cheese, sugar, salt and Italian seasoning in medium bowl; mix well. Combine buttermilk and oil in separate bowl, mix well. Place dry ingredients and buttermilk mixture in bread machine pan according to manual.

Select white bread and light crust settings. Remove bread from pan to wire rack. Cool completely before slicing.

MAKES 1 LOAF (16 SERVINGS)

tip

Refrigerated ingredients (except eggs) can be warmed to room temperature quickly by microwaving them for 15 to 20 seconds on HIGH.

TANGY
BUTTERMILK CHEESE
BREAD

2½ teaspoons/12.5 mL quick-rising yeast

2¾ cups/675 mL bread flour

1 cup/250 mL **Quaker® 100% Whole Grain Large Flake Oats** or **Quaker® 100% Whole Grain Quick Oats** (uncooked)

2 tablespoons/30 mL granulated sugar

1½ teaspoons/7.5 mL salt

¾ cup/175 mL (3 ounces/ 90 grams) shredded sharp Cheddar cheese

1⅓ cups/325 mL buttermilk

Bring all refrigerated ingredients to room temperature by letting them stand on counter about 30 minutes.

Place yeast in bread machine pan according to directions in manual.

Combine flour, oats, sugar and salt in medium bowl; mix well. Stir in Cheddar cheese. Place dry ingredients and buttermilk in bread machine pan according to manual.

Select white bread and light crust settings. Remove bread from pan to wire rack. Cool completely before slicing.

MAKES 1 LOAF (16 SERVINGS)

tip

If buttermilk is unavailable, substitute soured milk. Combine 4 teaspoons/20 mL vinegar or lemon juice with enough milk to equal 1⅓ cups/325 mL. Stir well. Let stand 5 minutes before using.

OATMEAL BREAD

2¼ teaspoons/11.25 mL quick-rising active dry yeast

3 cups/750 mL bread flour

1 cup/250 mL **Quaker® 100% Whole Grain Large Flake Oats** or **Quaker® 100% Whole Grain Quick Oats** (uncooked)

2 tablespoons/30 mL granulated sugar

1 teaspoon/5 mL salt

1¼ cups/300 mL milk or water

2 tablespoons/30 mL butter or margarine, melted, or 1 tablespoon/15 mL vegetable oil

Bring all refrigerated ingredients to room temperature by letting them stand on counter for about 30 minutes.

Place yeast in bread machine according to directions in manual.

Combine flour, oats, sugar and salt in medium bowl; mix well. Combine milk and butter in separate bowl; mix well. Place dry ingredients and milk mixture into bread machine pan according to manual.

Select white bread and light crust settings. Remove bread from pan to wire rack. Cool completely before slicing.

MAKES 1 LOAF (16 SERVINGS)

MAPLE FRUIT OATMEAL BREAD: Decrease milk to 1 cup/250 mL. Combine with margarine and ⅓ cup/75 mL Aunt Jemima® Original Syrup. Proceed as recipe directs. Add ½ cup/125 mL chopped dried fruit to dough partway through kneading cycle as directed in manual.

WHOLE WHEAT OATMEAL BREAD: Decrease bread flour to 1½ cups/350 mL; add 1½ cups/350 mL whole wheat flour. Proceed as recipe directs.

tip

Refrigerated ingredients (except eggs) can be warmed to room temperature quickly by microwaving them for 15 to 20 seconds on HIGH.

LET 'EM
EAT CAKE

SNOW CAKES

1 box (18.25 ounces/515 grams) white cake mix without pudding

4 egg whites

1 cup/250 mL (8 ounces/225 grams) low fat vanilla yogurt*

½ cup/125 mL water

⅓ cup/75 mL vegetable oil

1 cup/250 mL **Quaker® 100% Whole Grain Large Flake Oats** or **Quaker® 100% Whole Grain Quick Oats** (uncooked)

1 quart/1 litre premium vanilla ice cream**

Yogurt containing gelatin is not recommended.

**Light/reduced-fat ice cream is not recommended.*

Heat oven to 350°F/180°C. Line 24 medium muffin pan cups with paper or foil baking cups.

Beat cake mix, egg whites, yogurt, water and oil in large bowl with electric mixer according to package directions. Gently fold in oats. Divide batter evenly among muffin cups, filling each about ¾ full.

Bake 20 minutes or until wooden pick inserted in centre comes out clean. Remove from pan, cool completely on wire rack.

Remove ice cream from freezer and allow to soften just enough so it can be mixed. Transfer to chilled bowl; stir just until ice cream is spreadable but still holds its shape. Working quickly, "frost" each cupcake with softened ice cream. Place frosted cupcakes on tray and return to freezer to firm up slightly, no more than 30 minutes.

MAKES 24 CUPCAKES

VARIATION: Sprinkle frosted cupcakes with shredded coconut.

MOCHA CHIP
CHEESECAKE
BARS

CRUST

½ cup/125 mL (1 stick) margarine or butter, softened

½ cup/125 mL firmly packed brown sugar

1¼ cups/300 mL **Quaker® 100% Whole Grain Large Flake Oats** or **Quaker® 100% Whole Grain Quick Oats** (uncooked)

1 cup/250 mL all-purpose flour

FILLING

3 packages (8 ounces/225 grams each) regular or reduced-fat cream cheese, softened

¾ cup/175 mL granulated sugar

2 tablespoons/30 mL instant coffee granules or espresso powder

1 tablespoon/15 mL unsweetened cocoa powder

1 teaspoon/5 mL vanilla extract

3 eggs

1 cup/250 mL semi-sweet chocolate chips, divided

Heat oven to 350°F/180°C.

For crust, beat margarine and brown sugar in medium bowl until creamy. Add oats and flour; mix well. Press dough evenly onto bottom of ungreased 13×9-inch baking pan. Bake 15 minutes. Cool on wire rack.

For filling, beat cream cheese, granulated sugar, coffee granules, cocoa and vanilla extract in large bowl with electric mixer at medium speed until smooth. Add eggs; beat just until well blended. Stir in ¾ cup/175 mL chocolate chips. Pour filling evenly over crust. Sprinkle with remaining ¼ cup/60 mL chocolate chips.

Bake 30 to 35 minutes or until centre is set. Cool completely in pan on wire rack. Cut into bars. Store tightly covered in refrigerator.

MAKES 16 BARS

APPLE
UPSIDE-DOWN
OAT CAKES

2 cans (4 ounces/120 grams each) spiced diced apples in light syrup

¼ cup/60 mL firmly packed brown sugar, divided

1½ cups/350 mL all-purpose flour

1 cup/250 mL **Quaker® 100% Whole Grain Large Flake Oats** or **Quaker® 100% Whole Grain Quick Oats** (uncooked)

½ cup/125 mL granulated sugar

1 tablespoon/15 mL baking powder

1 teaspoon/5 mL ground cinnamon

⅛ teaspoon/0.625 mL ground nutmeg

1 cup/250 mL unsweetened apple juice

¼ cup/60 mL vegetable oil

1 egg, lightly beaten

Heat oven to 400°F/200°C. Spray bottoms and sides of 12 medium muffin pan cups with nonstick cooking spray.

Drain apples, reserving syrup. Spoon 5 to 6 apple pieces in single layer onto bottom of each muffin pan cup. Top each with ½ teaspoon/2.5 mL reserved apple syrup and 1 teaspoon/5 mL brown sugar.

Combine flour, oats, granulated sugar, baking powder, cinnamon and nutmeg in large bowl; mix well. Combine apple juice, oil and egg in medium bowl; mix well. Add to oat mixture; mix just until dry ingredients are moistened. Divide batter evenly among muffin cups.

Bake 16 to 19 minutes or until golden brown. Cool 5 minutes in pan on wire rack. Use narrow metal spatula to loosen edges of cakes from sides of muffin cups. Place baking sheet on top of muffin pan and invert. Carefully lift off muffin pan. Serve warm.

MAKES 12 SERVINGS

CARAMEL-TOPPED CHEESECAKES WITH OAT-PECAN CRUST

CRUST

1½ cups/350 mL **Quaker® 100% Whole Grain Large Flake Oats** or **Quaker® 100% Whole Grain Quick Oats** (uncooked)

½ cup/125 mL finely chopped pecans

½ cup/125 mL firmly packed light brown sugar

¼ cup/60 mL (½ stick) butter or margarine, melted

FILLING

2 packages (8 ounces/225 grams each) cream cheese, softened

¾ cup/175 mL firmly packed light brown sugar

1 teaspoon/5 mL vanilla extract

3 large eggs, at room temperature

½ cup/125 mL sour cream

¾ cup/175 mL butterscotch caramel topping

Sea salt

Heat oven to 375°F/190°C. Line 18 medium muffin pan cups with foil liners.

For crust, combine oats, pecans, ½ cup/125 mL brown sugar and butter in large bowl, blending well. Spoon about 2 tablespoons/30 mL of mixture into bottom of each foil-lined muffin cup, then press evenly and firmly to form crust. Bake 8 to 10 minutes, or until golden brown. Remove from oven and cool.

Reduce oven temperature to 325°F/160°C. For filling, beat cream cheese in large bowl with electric mixer at medium-high speed until light and fluffy, scraping bowl occasionally. Add ¾ cup/175 mL brown sugar and vanilla extract; blend well. Add eggs, one at a time, beating just until blended. Add sour cream; mix well. Divide batter evenly among muffin cups. Bake 20 to 22 minutes, or just until set. Cool in pans on wire rack. Chill at least 2 hours.

Top each individual cheesecake, just before serving, with scant tablespoon/ 15 mL of butterscotch caramel topping (if too thick to spread, heat in microwave a few seconds to soften). Sprinkle on a few grains of sea salt and serve.

MAKES 18 CHEESECAKES

ORANGE CRANBERRY UPSIDE-DOWN CAKE

1 cup/250 mL granulated sugar, divided

½ cup/125 mL water

2 tablespoons/30 mL cornstarch

1½ cups/350 mL fresh or frozen (not thawed) cranberries

2 oranges, peeled, sliced and cut in half

4 teaspoons/20 mL grated orange peel, divided

1 cup/250 mL all-purpose flour

1 tablespoon/15 mL baking powder

½ cup/125 mL (1 stick) margarine or butter

1 cup/250 mL **Quaker® 100% Whole Grain Large Flake Oats or Quaker® 100% Whole Grain Quick Oats** (uncooked)

½ cup/125 mL fat-free (skim) milk

2 egg whites, lightly beaten

Heat oven to 400°F/200°C.

Combine ⅔ cup/150 mL sugar, water and cornstarch in medium saucepan; mix well. Stir in cranberries. Heat to a boil; reduce heat. Simmer 2 minutes or until thickened. Stir in oranges and 2 teaspoons/10 mL orange peel. Spread into 9-inch quiche dish or 9-inch square baking pan.

Combine flour, baking powder, remaining ⅓ cup/75 mL sugar and remaining 2 teaspoons/10 mL orange peel in large bowl; mix well. Cut in margarine with pastry blender or two knives until crumbly. Stir in oats, milk and egg whites, mixing until moistened. Spread over fruit.

Bake 28 to 35 minutes or until golden brown. Cool 15 minutes in pan on wire rack. Invert onto serving platter. Serve warm.

MAKES 12 TO 16 SERVINGS

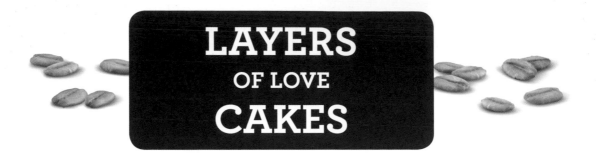

LAYERS
OF LOVE
CAKES

CUPCAKES

1 package (18.25 ounces/515 grams) white cake mix, regular or with pudding

1½ cups/350 mL fat-free (skim) milk

⅓ cup/75 mL canola oil

3 large egg whites

1 teaspoon/5 mL vanilla extract

1 cup/250 mL **Quaker® 100% Whole Grain Large Flake Oats or Quaker® 100% Whole Grain Quick Oats** (uncooked)

FILLING

2 ounces/60 grams reduced-fat cream cheese, softened

3 tablespoons/45 mL powdered sugar, plus additional for garnish

½ teaspoon/2.5 mL vanilla extract

1 cup/250 mL whipping cream

1¾ cups/450 mL fresh or frozen raspberries, coarsely crushed

Heat oven to 350°F/180°C. Lightly spray 24 medium muffin pan cups with nonstick cooking spray.

For cupcakes, beat cake mix, milk, oil, egg whites and 1 teaspoon/5 mL vanilla extract in large bowl with electric mixer at low speed 30 seconds to blend. Beat 2 minutes on medium speed, scraping bowl occasionally. Gently fold in oats. Divide batter evenly among muffin cups, filling each about ¾ full.

Bake 20 to 22 minutes or until wooden pick inserted in centre comes out clean. Cool 2 minutes in pan. Remove from pan; cool completely on wire rack.

For filling, beat cream cheese, powdered sugar and ½ teaspoon/2.5 mL vanilla extract with electric mixer at low speed until blended. Add whipping cream, gradually increasing mixer speed to high and beating until soft peaks form. (Do not overbeat.)

Slice cupcakes in half horizontally with serrated knife. Spread cut side of cupcake bottoms with heaping measuring teaspoonful/5 mL crushed raspberries. Top with heaping measuring tablespoonful/15 mL filling. Place cupcake tops, cut sides down, on top of filling, pressing gently. Sprinkle with powdered sugar and garnish with additional fresh berries if desired. Cover and refrigerate leftover cupcakes up to three days.

MAKES 24 CUPCAKES

tip

Cupcakes may be baked ahead and frozen in tightly covered container up to one month. To thaw, remove cupcakes from container to plate and let stand at room temperature 30 minutes.

HIDDEN
BERRY
CUPCAKES

1¾ cups/450 mL all-purpose flour

1¼ cups/300 mL granulated sugar

1 tablespoon/15 mL baking powder

½ teaspoon/2.5 mL salt

⅓ cup/75 mL (⅔ stick) butter, softened

3 eggs

⅔ cup/150 mL milk

1 tablespoon/15 mL vanilla extract

1 cup/250 mL **Quaker® 100% Whole Grain Large Flake Oats** or **Quaker® 100% Whole Grain Quick Oats** (uncooked)

½ cup/125 mL seedless strawberry or raspberry fruit spread

Powdered sugar

Heat oven to 350°F/180°C. Line 16 medium muffin pan cups with foil or paper liners.

Combine flour, granulated sugar, baking powder and salt in large bowl. Add butter and beat with electric mixer at low speed until crumbly, about 1 minute. Combine eggs, milk and vanilla extract in medium bowl; add to flour mixture. Beat on low speed until incorporated, then on medium speed 2 minutes. Gently fold in oats. Divide batter evenly among muffin cups, filling each about ¾ full.

Bake 18 minutes or until a wooden pick inserted in centre comes out clean. Remove from pan; cool completely on wire rack.

Cut cone-shaped piece with small sharp knife from centre of each cupcake, leaving ¾-inch border around edge of cupcake. Carefully remove and reserve cake pieces. Fill each depression with generous teaspoon/5 mL of fruit spread. Top with reserved cake pieces; sift powdered sugar over tops of cupcakes.

MAKES 16 CUPCAKES

DOUBLE GINGER OAT BARS

BARS

- 6 tablespoons/90 mL butter or light butter
- ⅔ cup/150 mL firmly packed brown sugar
- 1 package (14.5 ounces/ 410 grams) gingerbread cake and cookie mix
- 1¼ cups/300 mL **Quaker® 100% Whole Grain Large Flake Oats or Quaker® 100% Whole Grain Quick Oats** (uncooked)
- ⅓ cup/75 mL water
- 1 large egg

FROSTING

- 4 ounces/120 grams reduced-fat cream cheese
- 2 tablespoons/30 mL butter or light butter
- 1½ cups/350 mL powdered sugar
- 2 tablespoons/30 mL finely chopped crystallized ginger or ½ teaspoon/2.5 mL ground ginger

  Red and green decorator icing (optional)

Heat oven to 350°F/180°C. Spray 13×9-inch metal baking pan with nonstick cooking spray.

For bars, melt 6 tablespoons/90 mL butter over low heat in large saucepan. Remove from heat. Add brown sugar; stir with wooden spoon until well blended. Add gingerbread mix, oats, water and egg; stir until well blended. Spread evenly in prepared pan.

Bake 30 to 33 minutes or until wooden pick inserted in centre comes out with a few moist crumbs clinging to it. Cool bars completely in pan on wire rack.*

For frosting, beat cream cheese and 2 tablespoons/30 mL butter in medium bowl with electric mixer until blended. Gradually add powdered sugar, beating until smooth. Beat in ginger.

Spread frosting evenly over bars. Cover and refrigerate until ready to cut and decorate.

To decorate, cut into bars and remove from pan. Using red and green icing, pipe ribbons, holly leaves and berries or other decorations onto each bar. Refrigerate, uncovered, until decorations set, then cover and refrigerate up to three days.

MAKES 42 BARS

*If desired, at this point bars can be frozen, covered, up to two months. Let thaw at room temperature about 30 minutes. Proceed as directed in steps 4 and 5. If desired, ¾ teaspoon/3.75 mL vanilla extract may be substituted for ginger in frosting.

APPLE SPICE CAKE

TOPPING

- 1 cup/250 mL **Quaker® 100% Whole Grain Large Flake Oats** or **Quaker® 100% Whole Grain Quick Oats** (uncooked)
- ½ cup/125 mL firmly packed brown sugar
- ½ teaspoon/2.5 mL ground cinnamon
- ¼ cup/60 mL (½ stick) butter, softened

CAKE

- 1 package (18.5 ounces/525 grams) spice cake mix
- 1 cup/250 mL **Quaker® 100% Whole Grain Large Flake Oats** or **Quaker® 100% Whole Grain Quick Oats** (uncooked)
- 1 cup/250 mL (8 ounces/225 grams) low fat plain yogurt
- 3 eggs
- ¼ cup/60 mL vegetable oil
- ¼ cup/60 mL water
- 1½ cups/350 mL finely chopped apples (about 2 medium)
- Whipped cream (optional)

Heat oven to 350°F/180°C. Spray 13×9-inch metal baking pan with nonstick cooking spray.

For topping, combine 1 cup/250 mL oats, brown sugar and cinnamon in medium bowl. Cut in butter with pastry blender or two knives until mixture resembles coarse crumbs. Set aside.

For cake, combine cake mix, 1 cup/250 mL oats, yogurt, eggs, oil and water in large bowl. Blend with electric mixer at low speed until moistened; mix at medium speed for 2 minutes. Stir in apples. Pour into pan. Sprinkle topping evenly over batter.

Bake 40 to 45 minutes or until wooden pick inserted in centre comes out clean. Serve warm or at room temperature with whipped cream, if desired.

MAKES 16 SERVINGS

GINGERBREAD CUPCAKES

CUPCAKES

1¾ cups/450 mL all-purpose flour

1 cup/250 mL **Quaker® 100% Whole Grain Large Flake Oats** or **Quaker® 100% Whole Grain Quick Oats** (uncooked)

⅓ cup/75 mL granulated sugar

1 tablespoon/15 mL ground ginger

1 teaspoon/5 mL baking soda

¾ teaspoon/3.75 mL ground cinnamon

½ teaspoon/2.5 mL salt (optional)

½ cup/125 mL fat-free (skim) milk

½ cup/125 mL molasses

⅓ cup/75 mL vegetable oil

1 egg, lightly beaten

GLAZE

1 cup/250 mL powdered sugar

3 to 4 teaspoons/15 to 20 mL lemon juice

½ teaspoon/2.5 mL grated lemon peel (optional)

Heat oven to 375°F/190°C. Line 12 medium muffin pan cups with paper baking cups.

Combine flour, oats, granulated sugar, ginger, baking soda, cinnamon and, if desired, salt in large bowl; mix well. Combine milk, molasses, oil and egg in medium bowl; mix well. Add to dry ingredients all at once; mix until well blended. Fill muffin cups almost full.

Bake 20 to 23 minutes or until wooden pick inserted in centre comes out clean. Remove from pan; cool completely on wire rack.

Combine glaze ingredients, adding enough lemon juice for desired consistency; mix until smooth. Drizzle glaze over cooled cupcakes. Store loosely covered.

MAKES 12 CUPCAKES

CHERRY ALMOND OATMEAL CAKE

TOPPING

- ¼ cup/60 mL **Quaker® 100% Whole Grain Large Flake Oats or Quaker® 100% Whole Grain Quick Oats** (uncooked)

- 2 tablespoons/30 mL all-purpose flour

- 2 tablespoons/30 mL firmly packed brown sugar

- ¼ teaspoon/1.25 mL ground nutmeg

- 1 tablespoon/15 mL margarine, chilled

- ¼ cup/60 mL sliced almonds

CAKE

- 1 container (8 ounces/225 grams) low fat cherry (fruit on the bottom) yogurt

- ½ cup/125 mL granulated sugar

- 4 egg whites or 2 eggs, beaten

- 3 tablespoons/45 mL margarine, melted

- 1 teaspoon/5 mL vanilla extract

- ½ teaspoon/2.5 mL almond extract

- 1½ cups/350 mL all-purpose flour

- 1 cup/250 mL **Quaker® 100% Whole Grain Large Flake Oats or Quaker® 100% Whole Grain Quick Oats** (uncooked)

- 2 teaspoons/10 mL baking powder

- ½ teaspoon/2.5 mL baking soda

- ¼ teaspoon/1.25 mL salt

- 1 cup/250 mL cherry pie filling, divided

Heat oven to 350°F/180°C. Lightly spray 8-inch square baking pan or 9-inch heart-shaped pan (2 inches deep) with nonstick cooking spray.

For topping, combine ¼ cup/60 mL oats, 2 tablespoons/30 mL flour, brown sugar and nutmeg; mix well. Cut in 1 tablespoon/15 mL margarine with pastry blender or two knives until mixture resembles coarse crumbs. Stir in almonds. Set aside.

For cake, combine yogurt, granulated sugar, egg whites, 3 tablespoons/45 mL margarine, vanilla extract and almond extract in large bowl; mix well. Add combined 1½ cups/350 mL flour, 1 cup/250 mL oats, baking powder, baking soda and salt; mix just until moistened. (Do not overmix.)

Spread half of batter in pan. Drop ½ cup/125 mL pie filling in small spoonfuls randomly over batter. Top with remaining batter. Drop spoonfuls of remaining pie filling over batter; sprinkle evenly with topping.

Bake 45 to 55 minutes or until wooden pick inserted in centre comes out clean. Cool on wire rack. Serve warm. Store cooled cake tightly covered at room temperature.

MAKES 12 SERVINGS

FUNNY FACE UPSIDE-DOWN CARROT-OAT CAKES

TOPPING

2 tablespoons/30 mL firmly packed brown sugar

1 tablespoon/15 mL melted butter

⅓ cup/75 mL crushed pineapple, well drained

Raisins or dried cranberries

Shredded carrots

CAKES

1¼ cups/300 mL all-purpose flour

1 cup/250 mL **Quaker® 100% Whole Grain Large Flake Oats** or **Quaker® 100% Whole Grain Quick Oats** (uncooked)

¾ cup/175 mL firmly packed brown sugar

2 teaspoons/10 mL baking powder

2 teaspoons/10 mL ground cinnamon

1 teaspoon/5 mL baking soda

¼ teaspoon/1.25 mL salt

1 egg

½ cup/125 mL low fat (2%) milk

⅓ cup/75 mL (⅔ stick) butter, melted

½ cup/125 mL packaged shredded carrots, chopped*

⅓ cup/75 mL crushed pineapple, well drained

⅓ cup/75 mL raisins or dried cranberries

Heat oven to 400°F/200°C. Spray 12 medium muffin pan cups with nonstick cooking spray.

For topping, combine 2 tablespoons/30 mL brown sugar and 1 tablespoon/15 mL melted butter in small bowl; divide evenly among muffin pan cups. Place pineapple, raisins and carrots in muffin cups. Use pineapple to make hair, raisins to make eyes and nose, and carrot shreds to make smiles or whiskers. Set aside.

For cakes, combine flour, oats, ¾ cup/175 mL brown sugar, baking powder, cinnamon, baking soda and salt in large bowl; mix well. Combine egg, milk and ⅓ cup/75 mL melted butter in separate bowl; mix well. Add to dry ingredients all at once; stir just until dry ingredients are moistened. Gently stir in ½ cup/125 mL carrots, ⅓ cup/75 mL pineapple and ⅓ cup/75 mL raisins. Divide batter evenly among muffin cups.

Bake 15 to 18 minutes or until golden brown. Cool 5 minutes in pan on wire rack. Loosen edges with thin metal spatula; invert cakes onto cooling rack, face side up. Serve warm or at room temperature. Store leftover cakes tightly wrapped at room temperature.

MAKES 12 SERVINGS

LAZY DAISY
OATMEAL CAKE

CAKE

- 1¼ cups/300 mL boiling water
- 1 cup/250 mL **Quaker® 100% Whole Grain Large Flake Oats or Quaker® 100% Whole Grain Quick Oats** (uncooked)
- 1 cup/250 mL granulated sugar
- 1 cup/250 mL firmly packed brown sugar
- 5 tablespoons/75 mL margarine or butter, softened
- 2 egg whites or 1 egg
- 1 teaspoon/5 mL vanilla extract
- 1¾ cups/450 mL all-purpose flour
- 1 teaspoon/5 mL baking soda
- 1 teaspoon/5 mL ground cinnamon
- ¼ teaspoon/1.25 mL ground nutmeg (optional)
- ¼ teaspoon/1.25 mL salt (optional)

TOPPING

- ½ cup/125 mL shredded coconut
- ½ cup/125 mL firmly packed brown sugar
- ½ cup/125 mL **Quaker® 100% Whole Grain Large Flake Oats or Quaker® 100% Whole Grain Quick Oats** (uncooked)
- 3 tablespoons/45 mL fat-free (skim) milk
- 2 tablespoons/30 mL margarine or butter, melted

Heat oven to 350°F/180°C. Lightly grease and flour 8- or 9-inch square baking pan.

For cake, pour boiling water over 1 cup/250 mL oats in medium bowl; mix well. Set aside.

Beat granulated sugar, 1 cup/250 mL brown sugar and 5 tablespoons/75 mL margarine in large bowl until well blended. Add egg whites and vanilla extract; beat well. Add reserved oat mixture and combined flour, baking soda, cinnamon, and, if desired, nutmeg and salt; mix well. Pour batter into prepared pan.

Bake 55 to 65 minutes for 8-inch pan, 50 to 60 minutes for 9-inch pan, or until wooden pick inserted in centre comes out clean. Transfer cake in pan to wire rack.

For topping, combine all ingredients in small bowl; mix well. Spread evenly over top of warm cake.

Broil about 4 inches from heat 1 to 2 minutes or until topping is bubbly. Watch closely; topping burns easily. Cool cake in pan on wire rack. Store tightly covered at room temperature.

MAKES 12 SERVINGS

PEANUT 'N' JELLY
MUFFIN CAKE

TOPPING

⅓ cup/75 mL **Quaker® 100% Whole Grain Large Flake Oats** or **Quaker® 100% Whole Grain Quick Oats** (uncooked)

¼ cup/60 mL all-purpose flour

2 tablespoons/30 mL firmly packed brown sugar

⅓ cup/75 mL peanut butter, chunky or creamy

1 tablespoon/15 mL stick margarine or butter, softened

CAKE

1½ cups/350 mL all-purpose flour*

1 cup/250 mL **Quaker® 100% Whole Grain Large Flake Oats** or **Quaker® 100% Whole Grain Quick Oats** (uncooked)

½ cup/125 mL firmly packed brown sugar

2 teaspoons/10 mL baking powder

¼ teaspoon/1.25 mL salt (optional)

1 cup/250 mL fat-free (skim) milk

¼ cup/60 mL (½ stick) margarine or butter, melted

1 egg, lightly beaten

1 teaspoon/5 mL vanilla extract

½ cup/125 mL grape, strawberry or raspberry jelly

*If using large flake oats, increase flour to 1⅔ cups/400 mL.

Heat oven to 350°F/180°C. Spray 9-inch round metal cake pan with nonstick cooking spray.

For topping, combine ⅓ cup/75 mL oats, ¼ cup/60 mL flour and 2 tablespoons/30 mL brown sugar in small bowl. Cut in peanut butter and softened margarine with two knives or fingertips until mixture is crumbly. Set aside.

For cake, combine 1½ cups/350 mL flour, 1 cup/250 mL oats, ½ cup/ 125 mL brown sugar, baking powder and, if desired, salt in large bowl; mix well. Combine milk, melted margarine, egg and vanilla extract in small bowl; blend well. Add to dry ingredients all at once; stir just until dry ingredients are moistened. (Do not overmix.) Pour into pan. Spoon jelly by teaspoonfuls/ 5 mL randomly over batter. Crumble reserved topping evenly over batter.

Bake 35 to 40 minutes or until golden brown and wooden pick inserted in centre comes out with just a few moist crumbs clinging to it. Cool 10 minutes in pan on wire rack. Cut into wedges; serve warm.

MAKES 10 SERVINGS

tip

Cake can be baked in an 8-inch round metal cake pan. Bake 40 to 45 minutes.

GINGER
OAT CRUMB
CAKE

TOPPING

- ⅓ cup/75 mL **Quaker® 100% Whole Grain Large Flake Oats or Quaker® 100% Whole Grain Quick Oats** (uncooked)
- ¼ cup/60 mL all-purpose flour
- ¼ cup/60 mL firmly packed brown sugar
- 2 to 3 tablespoons/30 to 45 mL finely chopped crystallized ginger or 1 teaspoon/5 mL ground ginger
- 3 tablespoons/45 mL margarine or butter, chilled and cut into pieces

CAKE

- 1¼ cups/300 mL boiling water
- 1 cup/250 mL **Quaker® 100% Whole Grain Large Flake Oats or Quaker® 100% Whole Grain Quick Oats** (uncooked)
- 1 cup/250 mL granulated sugar
- 1 cup/250 mL firmly packed brown sugar
- 5 tablespoons/75 mL margarine or butter, softened
- 2 egg whites
- 1 teaspoon/5 mL vanilla extract
- 1¾ cups/450 mL all-purpose flour
- 1 tablespoon/15 mL ground ginger
- 1 teaspoon/5 mL ground cinnamon
- 1 teaspoon/5 mL baking soda
- ½ teaspoon/2.5 mL ground cloves
- ¼ teaspoon/1.25 mL salt (optional)

Heat oven to 350°F/180°C. Lightly grease and flour 9-inch square or 11×7-inch baking pan.

For topping, combine ⅓ cup/75 mL oats, ¼ cup/60 mL flour, ¼ cup/ 60 mL brown sugar and crystallized ginger in small bowl; mix well. Cut in 3 tablespoons/45 mL margarine with pastry blender or two knives until mixture is crumbly. Set aside.

For cake, pour boiling water over 1 cup/250 mL oats in medium bowl; mix well. Beat granulated sugar, 1 cup/250 mL brown sugar and 5 tablespoons/ 75 mL margarine in large bowl until well blended. Add egg whites and vanilla extract; beat well. Add oat mixture and combined 1¾ cups/450 mL flour, ground ginger, cinnamon, baking soda, cloves and, if desired, salt; stir just until dry ingredients are moistened. (Do not overmix.) Pour batter into prepared pan. Sprinkle with reserved topping.

Bake 50 to 60 minutes or until wooden pick inserted in centre comes out clean. Cool in pan on wire rack. Serve warm or at room temperature.

MAKES 12 SERVINGS

WHAT'S FOR DESSERT?

QUEEN OF HEARTS
FROZEN BERRY TART

1¼ cups/300 mL **Quaker® 100% Whole Grain Large Flake Oats** or **Quaker® 100% Whole Grain Quick Oats** (uncooked)

½ cup/125 mL all-purpose flour

⅓ cup/75 mL unsweetened cocoa powder

⅓ cup/75 mL firmly packed brown sugar

¼ cup/60 mL finely chopped almonds

½ cup/125 mL (1 stick) margarine or butter, melted

1 quart/1 litre vanilla ice cream

2 cups/500 mL raspberry or strawberry sorbet

1 cup/250 mL fresh raspberries or 1 package (10 ounces/285 grams) frozen raspberries in syrup, thawed

Heat oven to 350°F/180°C. Lightly spray 9-inch springform pan with nonstick cooking spray.

Combine oats, flour, cocoa, brown sugar and almonds in large bowl; mix well. Add margarine; mix well (mixture will be crumbly). Press oat mixture firmly onto bottom and about 1 inch up sides of pan.

Bake 11 to 12 minutes or until centre feels firm but springs back when lightly touched. Place pan on wire rack; cool completely.

Soften ice cream and sorbet by placing at room temperature 10 to 15 minutes. (Sorbet will soften faster than ice cream.) Spoon ice cream and sorbet onto cooled crust, alternating spoonfuls of ice cream and sorbet. Using spoon or knife, swirl ice cream and sorbet together, creating marbled effect. Smooth top of dessert. Cover and freeze until firm, about 4 hours, or up to three days.

Remove dessert from freezer 10 to 15 minutes before serving. Cut into wedges using sharp knife. Spoon raspberries over individual servings. Store tightly covered in freezer.

MAKES 8 SERVINGS

BANANA
PUDDING
PARFAITS

1 package (4-serving size) instant vanilla pudding mix

2 cups/500 mL cold low fat (2%) milk

2 medium ripe bananas, cut into ⅛-inch slices

2½ cups/600 mL **Quaker® Life® Original Cereal**

Whipped topping (optional)

Prepare pudding mix according to package directions using 2 cups/ 500 mL milk.

Layer 2 tablespoons/30 mL pudding, 4 to 5 banana slices and ¼ cup/ 60 mL cereal in 12-ounce/375-mL glass. Repeat layers. Top with 3 tablespoons/45 mL pudding, 2 tablespoons/30 mL cereal and, if desired, whipped topping.

Repeat, using remaining ingredients to make three more parfaits. Serve immediately.

MAKES 4 SERVINGS

SUBSTITUTION: Substitute 5 ready-to-eat vanilla pudding cups (3.5 ounces/100 mL each) for prepared instant pudding mix.

VARIATIONS:
- Substitute chocolate, banana or butterscotch pudding mix for vanilla.
- Substitute Quaker® Life® Toasted Cinnamon Cereal.
- For mini parfaits, divide ingredients evenly among eight 6-ounce/175 mL clear plastic cups.

FRUIT CRISP

FILLING

6 cups/1.5 litres peeled, thinly sliced apples, peaches or pears (6 to 8 medium)

¼ cup/60 mL water

¼ cup/60 mL firmly packed brown sugar

2 tablespoons/30 mL all-purpose flour

½ teaspoon/2.5 mL ground cinnamon

TOPPING

¾ cup/175 mL **Quaker® 100% Whole Grain Large Flake Oats** or **Quaker® 100% Whole Grain Quick Oats** (uncooked)

3 tablespoons/45 mL firmly packed brown sugar

2 tablespoons/30 mL margarine, melted

¼ teaspoon/1.25 mL ground cinnamon

Fat-free frozen yogurt (optional)

tip

If using apples, Jonathan, McIntosh, Winesap, Granny Smith, Northern Spy, Greening and Rome Beauty are recommended. One medium apple yields about 1 cup/250 mL sliced or chopped. If using pears, Bartlett, Anjou and Bosc are recommended.

Heat oven to 350°F/180°C. Spray 8-inch square glass baking dish with nonstick cooking spray.

For filling, combine fruit and water in large bowl. Add ¼ cup/60 mL brown sugar, flour and ½ teaspoon/2.5 mL cinnamon; stir until fruit is evenly coated. Spoon into baking dish.

For topping, combine oats, 3 tablespoons/45 mL brown sugar, margarine and ¼ teaspoon/1.25 mL cinnamon in medium bowl; mix well. Sprinkle evenly over fruit.

Bake 30 to 35 minutes or until fruit is tender. Serve warm with frozen yogurt, if desired.

MAKES 8 SERVINGS

EASY
APPLE CUSTARD
PIE

CRUST

1¼   cups/300 mL all-purpose flour

¾   cup/175 mL **Quaker® 100% Whole Grain Large Flake Oats or Quaker® 100% Whole Grain Quick Oats** (uncooked)

¼   cup/60 mL firmly packed brown sugar

⅛   teaspoon/0.625 salt (optional)

½   cup/125 mL (1 stick) margarine or butter, melted

1   tablespoon/15 mL water

1   teaspoon/5 mL vanilla extract

FILLING

1   container (8 ounces/225 grams) reduced-fat or regular sour cream

⅔   cup/150 mL firmly packed brown sugar

¼   cup/60 mL all-purpose flour

4   egg whites or 2 eggs, lightly beaten

½   teaspoon/2.5 mL ground cinnamon

⅛   teaspoon/0.625 ground nutmeg

4   cups/1 litre thinly sliced peeled apples (4 to 5 medium)

TOPPING

¼   cup/60 mL **Quaker® 100% Whole Grain Large Flake Oats or Quaker® 100% Whole Grain Quick Oats** (uncooked)

¼   cup/60 mL firmly packed brown sugar

¼   cup/60 mL all-purpose flour

¼   cup/60 mL (½ stick) margarine or butter, chilled and cut into pieces

Heat oven to 375°F/190°C. For crust, combine flour, oats, brown sugar and, if desired, salt in medium bowl; mix well. Add margarine, water and vanilla extract; mix well. Press firmly onto bottom and up sides of 9-inch glass pie plate, forming ¼-inch rim around edge. Bake 12 to 15 minutes or until light golden brown. Cool completely on wire rack.

For filling, combine sour cream, brown sugar, flour, egg whites, cinnamon and nutmeg in medium bowl. Add apples; mix well. Spoon into cooled crust.

For topping, combine oats, brown sugar and flour in medium bowl; mix well. Cut in margarine with pastry blender or two knives until mixture resembles coarse crumbs. Sprinkle over filling.

Bake 50 to 60 minutes or until knife inserted in centre comes out clean. Cool on wire rack. Serve warm or chilled. Store, tightly covered, in refrigerator.

MAKES 8 SERVINGS

PEACHY
BANANA-CRANBERRY
CRISP

FILLING

- 1 large ripe banana, peeled and sliced
- 1 tablespoon/15 mL lemon juice
- 2 packages (16 ounces/454 grams each) frozen sliced peaches, thawed (reserve liquid)
- ½ cup/125 mL dried cranberries
- ¼ teaspoon/1.25 mL almond extract
- ¼ cup/60 mL firmly packed brown sugar
- 2 tablespoons/30 mL all-purpose flour

TOPPING

- 1 cup/250 mL **Quaker® 100% Whole Grain Large Flake Oats** or **Quaker® 100% Whole Grain Quick Oats** (uncooked)
- ⅓ cup/75 mL sliced almonds
- ¼ cup/60 mL firmly packed brown sugar
- ¼ teaspoon/1.25 mL ground cinnamon
- 4 tablespoons/60 mL vegetable oil

  Low-fat vanilla yogurt, frozen yogurt or reduced-fat ice cream (optional)

Heat oven to 350°F/180°C.

For filling, combine banana and lemon juice in large bowl; mix well. Add peaches, cranberries, almond extract and reserved peach liquid; stir well. Combine ¼ cup/60 mL brown sugar and flour; add to fruit and mix until evenly coated. Spoon into 8-inch square glass baking dish.

For topping, combine all ingredients in small bowl; mix well. Sprinkle evenly over fruit in baking dish.

Bake 30 to 35 minutes or until filling is bubbly and topping is golden brown. If desired, serve warm with low fat vanilla yogurt for breakfast or with frozen yogurt or reduced-fat ice cream for dessert.

MAKES 10 SERVINGS

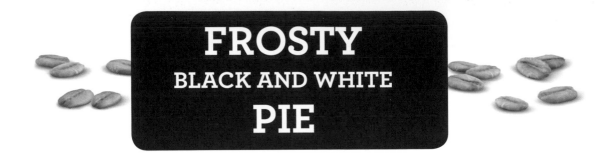

FROSTY
BLACK AND WHITE
PIE

1   cup/250 mL semi-sweet chocolate chips

1   tablespoon/15 mL solid vegetable shortening

2½ cups/600 mL **Quaker® Life® Original Cereal**, coarsely crushed

3   cups/750 mL vanilla ice cream, softened

3   cups/750 mL chocolate ice cream, softened

Line 9-inch glass pie plate or metal pie pan with aluminum foil.

Melt chocolate chips and vegetable shortening according to package directions. Combine melted chocolate and cereal in large bowl; mix until well coated. Remove ¼ cup/60 mL and spread on waxed paper; refrigerate. Press remaining cereal mixture onto bottom and up sides of pie plate. Refrigerate 30 minutes or until crust is firm.

Life crust carefully out of pie plate, peel off foil and return crust to pie plate. Spoon ice creams alternately into crust. Swirl together with spoon; smooth top. Crumble reserved chocolate-covered cereal; sprinkle over top of pie, gently pressing into ice cream. Cover pie, freeze until solid, at least 3 hours.

Remove pie from freezer 15 minutes before serving. Cut into wedges.

MAKES 8 SERVINGS

VARIATIONS:
- Substitute your favorite ice cream or frozen yogurt flavours for the vanilla and chocolate ice creams.
- Substitute Quaker® Life® Toasted Cinnamon Cereal for Original Cereal.

CINNAMON APPLE CRUMBLE

- 4 cups/1 litre peeled, cored and thinly sliced baking apples (about 2 large)
- 3 tablespoons/45 mL **Tropicana Pure Premium**® orange juice or **Dole**® 100% orange juice
- ¼ cup/60 mL granulated sugar
- 1 tablespoon/15 mL cornstarch
- 1 teaspoon/5 mL vanilla extract
- 1 teaspoon/5 mL ground cinnamon, divided
- ½ cup/125 mL firmly packed brown sugar
- ¼ cup/60 mL all-purpose flour
- ¼ cup/60 mL (½ stick) margarine or butter
- ½ cup/125 mL **Quaker**® **100% Whole Grain Large Flake Oats** or **Quaker**® **100% Whole Grain Quick Oats** (uncooked)

Heat oven to 400°F/200°C. Lightly grease 2-quart/2-litre baking dish.

Combine apples and orange juice in large bowl. Stir in granulated sugar, cornstarch, vanilla extract and ½ teaspoon/2.5 mL cinnamon; toss to coat. Spoon mixture into baking dish.

Combine brown sugar, flour and remaining ½ teaspoon/2.5 mL cinnamon in medium bowl; mix well. Cut in margarine with pastry blender or two knives until mixture resembles coarse crumbs; stir in oats. Sprinkle over apple mixture.

Bake 25 to 30 minutes or until topping is golden brown and apples are tender. Serve warm or at room temperature.

MAKES 6 SERVINGS

AUTUMN FRUIT COBBLER

3   large apples, cored and cut into ¼-inch wedges

2   medium-firm ripe Bartlett or Bosc pears, peeled,
     quartered and cored

⅓   cup/75 mL dried cranberries

1   cup/250 mL firmly packed light brown sugar, divided

2   tablespoons/30 mL cornstarch

1½ teaspoons/7.5 mL ground cinnamon, divided

1½ cups/350 mL all-purpose flour

1   cup/250 mL **Quaker® 100% Whole Grain Large Flake Oats
     or Quaker® 100% Whole Grain Quick Oats** (uncooked)

2   teaspoons/10 mL baking powder

¼   teaspoon/1.25 mL salt

½   cup/125 mL (1 stick) margarine or butter, chilled

⅔   cup/150 mL low fat (2%) milk

    Vanilla ice cream (optional)

Heat oven to 400°F/200°C.

Combine apples, pears and cranberries in large bowl. Combine ¾ cup/175 mL brown sugar, cornstarch and 1 teaspoon/5 mL cinnamon in small bowl; mix well. Add to fruit; mix well. Spoon into 2½-quart/2.5-litre glass baking dish. Bake, uncovered, 30 minutes.

Combine flour, oats, remaining ¼ cup/60 mL brown sugar, baking powder, salt and remaining ½ teaspoon/2.5 mL cinnamon in large bowl; mix well. Cut in margarine with pastry blender or two knives until mixture resembles coarse crumbs. Add milk; mix with fork until soft dough forms.

Turn out onto lightly floured surface; knead gently 6 to 8 times. Pat dough into ½-inch-thick rectangle. Cut with floured biscuit or cookie cutter.

Remove baking dish from oven; stir fruit. Carefully arrange biscuits over hot fruit; press lightly into fruit. Bake 15 to 20 minutes or until biscuits are golden brown and fruit mixture is bubbly. Serve warm with vanilla ice cream, if desired. Cover and refrigerate leftovers.

MAKES 8 SERVINGS

HARVEST MOON CRUMBLE PIE

CRUST

1 E-Z Oat Crust (recipe follows)

TOPPING

⅓ cup/75 mL **Quaker® 100% Whole Grain Large Flake Oats** or **Quaker® 100% Whole Grain Quick Oats** (uncooked)

¼ cup/60 mL all-purpose flour

¼ cup/60 mL firmly packed brown sugar

3 tablespoons/45 mL margarine or butter, chilled

FILLING

2 cans (21 ounces/595 mL each) apple or peach pie filling

½ cup/125 mL raisins

½ teaspoon/2.5 mL ground cinnamon

Whipped cream, ice cream or frozen yogurt (optional)

Prepare E-Z Oat Crust. Heat oven to 375°F/190°C.

For topping, combine oats, flour and brown sugar in small bowl; mix well. Cut in margarine using pastry blender or two knives until mixture is crumbly. Set aside.

For filling, combine pie filling, raisins and cinnamon in large bowl; mix well. Pour into prepared crust. Sprinkle reserved topping evenly over filling.

Bake 25 to 30 minutes or until topping is golden brown. Serve with whipped cream, ice cream or frozen yogurt, if desired.

MAKES 8 SERVINGS

E-Z OAT CRUST

1 cup/250 mL **Quaker® 100% Whole Grain Large Flake Oats** or **Quaker® 100% Whole Grain Quick Oats** (uncooked)

¼ cup/60 mL firmly packed brown sugar

¾ cup/175 mL all-purpose flour

½ cup/125 mL (1 stick) margarine or butter, melted

Heat oven to 375°F/190°C. Lightly spray 9-inch glass pie plate with nonstick cooking spray.

Combine all ingredients in large bowl; mix well. Press mixture evenly onto bottom and up sides of prepared pie plate.

Bake 12 to 15 minutes or until golden brown. Fill baked pie crust with desired filling.

MAKES ONE 9-INCH PIE CRUST

tip

To freeze baked pie crust, wrap in heavyweight plastic wrap or aluminum foil or place in plastic freezer bag or airtight container. Label, date and store in freezer up to 4 months. To thaw baked crust, unwrap frozen crust; let stand at room temperature. Or place unwrapped crust in 350°F/180°C oven about 5 minutes.

BUTTERSCOTCH APPLE CRISP

FILLING

2½ pounds/1.1 kg tart apples (about 6 medium), peeled and thinly sliced

1⅔ cups/400 mL (11 ounces/310 grams) butterscotch chips

¼ cup/60 mL firmly packed brown sugar

¼ cup/60 mL all-purpose flour

½ teaspoon/2.5 mL ground cinnamon

TOPPING

½ cup/125 mL all-purpose flour

¼ cup/60 mL firmly packed brown sugar

¼ cup/60 mL (½ stick) butter or margarine

1 cup/250 mL chopped nuts

¾ cup/175 mL **Quaker® 100% Whole Grain Large Flake Oats** or **Quaker® 100% Whole Grain Quick Oats** (uncooked)

Ice cream or whipped cream (optional)

Heat oven to 375°F/190°C.

For filling, arrange apples in 13×9-inch metal baking pan. Combine butterscotch chips, ¼ cup/60 mL brown sugar, ¼ cup/60 mL flour and cinnamon in small bowl; mix well. Sprinkle over apples.

Bake 20 minutes; remove from oven.

For topping, combine ½ cup/125 mL flour and ¼ cup/60 mL brown sugar in medium bowl. Cut in butter with pastry blender or two knives until crumbly. Stir in nuts and oats; sprinkle over apple layer. Bake 30 to 40 minutes or until apples are tender and topping is lightly browned. Cool slightly. Serve warm with ice cream, if desired.

MAKES 10 TO 12 SERVINGS

EASY
APPLE-BERRY
CRUMBLE PIE

1½ cups/350 mL **Quaker® 100% Whole Grain Large Flake Oats** or **Quaker® 100% Whole Grain Quick Oats** (uncooked)

1 cup/250 mL all-purpose flour

½ cup/125 mL firmly packed brown sugar

½ teaspoon/2.5 mL baking soda

10 tablespoons/150 mL butter or margarine, melted

1 can (21 ounces/595 mL) apple pie filling

¾ cup/175 mL dried cranberries

1¼ teaspoons/6.25 mL lemon juice

½ teaspoon/2.5 mL ground cinnamon

Heat oven to 375°F/190°C. Lightly spray 8- or 9-inch glass pie plate with nonstick cooking spray.

Combine oats, flour, brown sugar and baking soda in medium bowl. Add melted butter; mix well. Set aside ¾ cup/175 mL oat mixture for topping. Press remaining oat mixture firmly onto bottom and up sides of pie plate.

Bake 10 to 12 minutes or until light golden brown. Cool slightly on wire rack.

Stir together pie filling, cranberries, lemon juice and cinnamon in same bowl. Spoon filling over hot crust, spreading evenly. Sprinkle reserved oat mixture evenly over filling. Bake 18 to 22 minutes or until topping is golden brown. Serve warm or at room temperature.

MAKES 8 SERVINGS

PEAR CINNAMON
OAT
CRUMBLE

FILLING

- 6 cups/1.5 litres peeled and thinly sliced firm-ripe pears or Granny Smith apples
- ¼ cup/60 mL water
- ¼ cup/60 mL firmly packed brown sugar
- 2 tablespoons/30 mL all-purpose flour
- ½ teaspoon/2.5 mL ground cinnamon

TOPPING

- 1 cup/250 mL **Quaker® 100% Whole Grain Large Flake Oats** or **Quaker® 100% Whole Grain Quick Oats** (uncooked)
- ½ cup/125 mL slivered almonds (optional)
- ¼ cup/60 mL firmly packed brown sugar
- ¼ cup/60 mL (½ stick) margarine or butter, melted
- ¼ teaspoon/1.25 mL ground cinnamon

  Vanilla ice cream or whipped cream (optional)

Heat oven to 350°F/180°C.

Combine pears and water in large bowl. Add ¼ cup/60 mL brown sugar, flour and ½ teaspoon/2.5 mL cinnamon; stir until fruit is evenly coated. Spoon into 8-inch square glass baking dish.

Combine all topping ingredients except ice cream in medium bowl; mix well. Sprinkle evenly over pears.

Bake 30 to 35 minutes or until pears are tender. Serve warm with ice cream or whipped cream, if desired.

MAKES 8 SERVINGS

CHERRY
BERRY
CRISPS

FILLING

- ½ cup/125 mL granulated sugar
- 1 tablespoon/15 mL cornstarch
- ½ cup/125 mL cranberry juice or **Tropicana Pure Premium**® orange juice
- 2 cans (16 ounces/454 grams each) pitted sour cherries, drained
- ⅓ cup/75 mL sweetened dried cranberries

TOPPING

- ¾ cup/175 mL **Quaker® 100% Whole Grain Large Flake Oats** or **Quaker® 100% Whole Grain Quick Oats** (uncooked)
- 3 tablespoons/45 mL firmly packed brown sugar
- 2 tablespoons/30 mL margarine or butter, melted
- 1 tablespoon/15 mL all-purpose flour
- ¼ teaspoon/1.25 mL ground cinnamon

Heat oven to 375°F/190°C.

For filling, stir together granulated sugar and cornstarch in medium saucepan. Gradually stir in cranberry juice, mixing well. Stirring constantly, bring to a boil over medium-high heat. Cook and stir 1 minute or until thickened and clear. Remove from heat; stir in cherries and cranberries. Spoon into six small (about 6-ounce/175 mL) ovenproof heart-shaped ramekins, custard cups or soufflé cups, dividing evenly.

For topping, combine oats, brown sugar, margarine, flour and cinnamon in small bowl; mix well. Sprinkle topping over each fruit cup, dividing evenly.

Bake 15 to 20 minutes or until topping is golden brown. Serve warm.

MAKES 6 SERVINGS

VARIATION: Spoon filling into an 8-inch square glass baking dish. Sprinkle evenly with topping. Bake 25 to 30 minutes or until topping is golden brown.

BEST BLUEBERRY CRISP

FILLING

2 tablespoons/30 mL granulated sugar or heat-stable sugar substitute equal to 2 tablespoons/30 mL sugar

1½ tablespoons/22.5 mL all-purpose flour

1 teaspoon/5 mL ground cinnamon

6 cups/1.5 litres fresh or frozen (partially thawed) blueberries

1 teaspoon/5 mL vanilla extract

TOPPING

1 cup/250 mL **Quaker® 100% Whole Grain Large Flake Oats** or **Quaker® 100% Whole Grain Quick Oats** (uncooked)

⅓ cup/75 mL coarsely chopped almonds

2 tablespoons/30 mL granulated sugar or heat-stable sugar substitute equal to 2 tablespoons/30 mL sugar

¼ cup/60 mL (½ stick) margarine, melted

½ teaspoon/2.5 mL ground cinnamon

Heat oven to 350°F/180°C. Spray 8-inch square glass baking dish with nonstick cooking spray.

For filling, combine 2 tablespoons/30 mL sugar, flour and 1 teaspoon/ 5 mL cinnamon in large bowl; mix well. Add blueberries and vanilla extract; stir until fruit is evenly coated. Spoon into baking dish.

For topping, combine all ingredients in small bowl; mix well. Sprinkle evenly over fruit.

Bake 35 to 40 minutes or until topping is golden and filling is bubbly. Serve warm.

MAKES 8 SERVINGS

FRUITED OATMEAL CRISP

½ cup/125 mL **Aunt Jemima® Original, Buttermilk Original, Complete** or **Buttermilk Complete Pancake & Waffle Mix**

½ cup/125 mL **Quaker® 100% Whole Grain Large Flake Oats** or **Quaker® 100% Whole Grain Quick Oats**, uncooked

⅓ cup/75 mL firmly packed brown sugar

¼ teaspoon/1.25 mL ground cinnamon

⅓ cup/75 mL margarine or butter, chilled and cut into 1-inch pieces

2 cans (20 to 21 ounces/567 to 595 mL each) apple, cherry or peach pie filling

Heat oven to 350°F/180°C.

Combine pancake mix, oats, brown sugar and cinnamon in medium bowl; mix well. Cut in margarine using pastry blender or two knives until mixture resembles coarse crumbs.

Spoon pie filling into 8- or 9-inch baking dish. Top pie filling evenly with pancake-oat mixture.

Bake 25 to 30 minutes or until golden brown. Serve warm with ice cream, if desired.

MAKES 9 SERVINGS

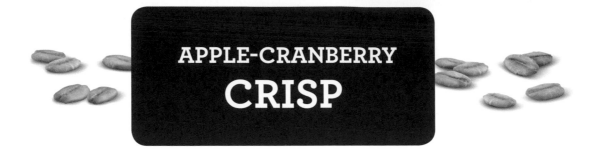

APPLE-CRANBERRY CRISP

FILLING

1½ tablespoons/22.5 mL all-purpose flour

1 tablespoon/15 mL granulated sugar

1 teaspoon/5 mL ground cinnamon

5 cups/1.25 litres peeled and sliced fresh apples (about 3 large, 1¼ pounds/565 grams)

¾ cup/175 mL fresh cranberries

½ cup/125 mL water

TOPPING

1 cup/250 mL **Quaker® 100% Whole Grain Large Flake Oats** or **Quaker® 100% Whole Grain Quick Oats** (uncooked)

¼ cup/60 mL coarsely chopped walnuts, pecans or almonds (optional)

1 tablespoon/15 mL granulated sugar

3 tablespoons/45 mL stick margarine, melted

½ teaspoon/2.5 mL ground cinnamon

Heat oven to 350°F/180°C. Spray 8-inch square glass baking dish with nonstick cooking spray.

For filling, combine flour, 1 tablespoon/15 mL sugar and 1 teaspoon/5 mL cinnamon in small bowl; mix well. Combine apples, cranberries and water in large bowl; mix well. Add cinnamon mixture to fruit; stir until fruit is evenly coated. Spoon into baking dish.

For topping, combine all ingredients in small bowl; mix well. Sprinkle evenly over fruit.

Bake 30 to 35 minutes or until apples feel tender when pierced with sharp knife. Serve warm.

MAKES 4 SERVINGS

VANISHING OATMEAL RAISIN COOKIE ICE CREAM SANDWICHES

1 cup/250 mL (2 sticks) margarine or butter, softened

1 cup/250 mL firmly packed brown sugar

½ cup/125 mL granulated sugar

2 eggs

1 teaspoon/5 mL vanilla extract

1½ cups/350 mL all-purpose flour

1 teaspoon/5 mL baking soda

1 teaspoon/5 mL ground cinnamon

½ teaspoon/2.5 mL salt (optional)

3 cups/750 mL **Quaker® 100% Whole Grain Large Flake Oats** or **Quaker® 100% Whole Grain Quick Oats** (uncooked)

1 cup/250 mL raisins

Softened ice cream or frozen yogurt

Heat oven to 350°F/180°C.

Beat together margarine, brown sugar and granulated sugar in large bowl with electric mixer until creamy. Add eggs and vanilla extract; beat well. Combine flour, baking soda, cinnamon and, if desired, salt; mix well. Add to margarine mixture; mix well. Stir in oats and raisins; mix well. Drop by rounded tablespoonfuls/15 mL portions onto ungreased cookie sheets.

Bake 10 to 12 minutes or until light golden brown. Cool 1 minute on cookie sheets; remove to wire racks. Cool completely. Store tightly covered.

Spread softened ice cream on bottom side of one cookie; top with second cookie to make sandwiches. Wrap airtight; freeze.

MAKES ABOUT 24 SANDWICHES

CHOCOLATE BLISS

CHOCOLATE LOVER'S OATMEAL

1¼ cups/300 mL chocolate milk or milk

⅔ cup/150 mL **Quaker® 100% Whole Grain Large Flake Oats** or **Quaker® 100% Whole Grain Quick Oats** (uncooked)

⅛ teaspoon/0.625 mL salt (optional)

1 tablespoon/15 mL semi-sweet chocolate chips

Bring milk just to a boil in medium saucepan. Stir in remaining ingredients. Cook about 1 minute for quick oats or 5 minutes for large flake oats, stirring occasionally.

MAKES 1 SERVING

MICROWAVE DIRECTIONS: For quick oats, combine all ingredients except chocolate pieces in 2-quart/2-litre microwave-safe bowl. Microwave 4 to 5 minutes on HIGH. Stir in chocolate chips; let stand 1 minute.

CHOCOLATE-CHERRY
THUMBPRINTS

- 2 cups/500 mL (12-ounce/360-gram package) semi-sweet chocolate chips, divided
- 1¾ cups/450 mL **Quaker® 100% Whole Grain Large Flake Oats** or **Quaker® 100% Whole Grain Quick Oats** (uncooked)
- 1½ cups/350 mL all-purpose flour
- ¼ cup/60 mL unsweetened cocoa powder
- 1 teaspoon/5 mL baking powder
- ¼ teaspoon/1.25 mL salt (optional)
- ¾ cup/175 mL granulated sugar
- ⅔ cup/150 mL butter or margarine, softened
- 2 large eggs
- 1 teaspoon/5 mL vanilla extract
- 2 cups/500 mL (two 10-ounce/285-gram jars) maraschino cherries, drained and patted dry

Microwave 1 cup/250 mL chocolate chips in small microwave-safe bowl 1 minute on HIGH; stir. Microwave at additional 10- to 20-second intervals, stirring until smooth.

Combine oats, flour, cocoa, baking powder and, if desired, salt in medium bowl; mix well. Beat sugar, butter, eggs and vanilla extract in large bowl with electric mixer until smooth. Beat in melted chocolate. Stir in oat mixture. Cover; refrigerate dough 1 hour.

Heat oven to 350°F/180°C. Shape dough into 1-inch balls. Place 2 inches apart on ungreased baking sheets. Press deep centres with thumb. Place maraschino cherry into each centre.

Bake 10 to 12 minutes or until set. Cool 2 minutes on baking sheets, remove to wire racks. Cool completely. Melt remaining 1 cup/250 mL chocolate chips; drizzle over cookies.

MAKES ABOUT 36 COOKIES

NOT-SO-SINFUL
BROWNIES

¼ cup/60 mL vegetable oil

3 squares (1 ounce/30 grams each) unsweetened chocolate

1¼ cups/300 mL granulated sugar

½ cup/125 mL applesauce

4 egg whites or 2 eggs, lightly beaten

1 teaspoon/5 mL vanilla extract

1 cup/250 mL **Quaker® 100% Whole Grain Large Flake Oats** or **Quaker® 100% Whole Grain Quick Oats** (uncooked)

1 cup/250 mL all-purpose flour

1 teaspoon/5 mL baking powder

¼ teaspoon/1.25 mL salt (optional)

1 tablespoon/15 mL powdered sugar

Heat oven to 350°F/180°C. Lightly spray bottom of 13×9-inch baking pan with nonstick cooking spray.

Heat oil and chocolate over low heat in large saucepan until chocolate is melted, stirring frequently. Remove from heat. Stir in granulated sugar and applesauce until sugar is dissolved. Stir in egg whites and vanilla extract until completely blended. Add combined oats, flour, baking powder and, if desired, salt; mix well. Spread evenly into pan.

Bake 22 to 25 minutes or until edges begin to pull away from sides of pan. Cool completely in pan on wire rack. Cut into bars. Store tightly covered. Sprinkle with powdered sugar just before serving.

MAKES 24 BARS

CHOCOLATE
CHUNK GRANOLA
BARS

1   cup/250 mL firmly packed brown sugar

⅔   cup/150 mL creamy peanut butter

½   cup/125 mL (1 stick) margarine or butter, softened

½   cup/125 mL light corn syrup

2   teaspoons/10 mL vanilla extract

3   cups/750 mL **Quaker® 100% Whole Grain Large Flake Oats** or **Quaker® 100% Whole Grain Quick Oats** (uncooked)

1½   bars (6 ounces/170 grams) sweet dark chocolate, chopped

¾   cup/175 mL shredded coconut

½   cup/125 mL raisins

⅓   cup/75 mL **Quaker® Kretschmer® Original** or **Honey Crunch Toasted Wheat Germ**

Heat oven to 350°F/180°C.

Beat brown sugar, peanut butter and margarine until fluffy. Add corn syrup and vanilla extract; mix well. Stir in oats, chocolate, coconut, raisins and wheat germ. Press onto bottom of ungreased 13×9-inch baking pan.

Bake 15 to 20 minutes or until light golden brown. Chill 1½ hours or until firm. Cut into bars. Store loosely covered.

MAKES 36 BARS

CHOCOLATE
BROWNIE
OATMEAL COOKIES

1 package (8 ounces/225 grams) cream cheese, softened

½ cup/125 mL (1 stick) margarine or butter, softened

1 cup/250 mL firmly packed brown sugar

½ cup/125 mL granulated sugar

2 eggs

½ teaspoon/2.5 mL vanilla extract

2 cups/500 mL (12 ounces/360 grams) semi-sweet chocolate chips, melted

1½ cups/350 mL all-purpose flour

1½ teaspoons/7.5 mL baking soda

3 cups/750 mL **Quaker® 100% Whole Grain Large Flake Oats** or **Quaker® 100% Whole Grain Quick Oats** (uncooked)

1 cup/250 mL chopped nuts

Powdered sugar (optional)

To melt chocolate chips, place in 1-quart/1-litre glass measuring cup or microwave-safe bowl. Microwave on HIGH 1 to 2 minutes or until melted and smooth, stirring every 30 seconds. Or place in top part of double boiler over hot—not boiling—water; stir occasionally until smooth.

Beat cream cheese, margarine and sugars in large bowl until creamy. Add eggs and vanilla extract; beat well. Add melted chocolate; mix well. Add combined flour and baking soda; mix well. Add oats and nuts; mix well. Cover; chill at least 1 hour.

Heat oven to 350°F/180°C. Shape dough into 1-inch balls. Place 3 inches apart on ungreased cookie sheets.

Bake 8 to 10 minutes or until cookies are almost set. (Centres should still be moist. Do not overbake.) Cool 1 minute on cookie sheets; remove to wire racks. Cool completely. Sprinkle with powdered sugar, if desired. Store tightly covered.

MAKES ABOUT 72 COOKIES

CHEWY
CHOCOLATE
NO-BAKES

1 cup/250 mL (6 ounces/ 170 grams) semi-sweet chocolate chips

5 tablespoons/75 mL light butter

14 large marshmallows

1 teaspoon/5 mL vanilla extract

2 cups/500 mL **Quaker® 100% Whole Grain Large Flake Oats or Quaker® 100% Whole Grain Quick Oats** (uncooked)

⅔ cup/150 mL (any combination of) raisins, diced dried mixed fruit, shredded coconut, miniature marshmallows or chopped nuts

Melt chocolate chips, butter and large marshmallows in large saucepan over low heat, stirring until smooth. Remove from heat; cool slightly. Stir in vanilla extract. Stir in oats and remaining ingredients.

Drop by rounded tablespoonfuls/ 15 mL onto waxed paper. Cover and refrigerate 2 to 3 hours. Let stand at room temperature about 15 minutes before serving. Store, tightly covered, in refrigerator.

MAKES ABOUT 36 TREATS

MICROWAVE DIRECTIONS:
Place chocolate chips, butter and marshmallows in large microwave-safe bowl. Microwave on HIGH 1 to 2 minutes or until mixture is melted and smooth, stirring every 30 seconds. Proceed as directed.

DALMATIAN CAKE

CAKE

- 1 package (18 ounces/510 grams) white cake mix
- 1¼ cups/300 mL **Quaker® 100% Whole Grain Large Flake Oats or Quaker® 100% Whole Grain Quick Oats** (uncooked)
- 1 cup/250 mL water
- ⅔ cup/150 mL whole or low fat (2%) milk
- 4 egg whites, lightly beaten
- 3 tablespoons/45 mL canola oil
- 1 teaspoon/5 mL vanilla extract
- ½ teaspoon/2.5 mL almond extract
- ¾ cup/175 mL mini semi-sweet chocolate chips

FROSTING

- 1 cup/250 mL powdered sugar
- ½ cup/125 mL (1 stick) butter or margarine, softened
- ⅓ cup/75 mL marshmallow cream
- ½ teaspoon/2.5 mL vanilla extract
- 1 cup/250 mL shredded coconut (optional)
- ¼ cup/60 mL mini semi-sweet chocolate chips

Heat oven to 350°F/180°C. Lightly grease or spray 13×9-inch metal baking pan with nonstick cooking spray.

Combine cake mix, oats, water, milk, egg whites, oil, 1 teaspoon/5 mL vanilla extract and almond extract in large bowl. Beat 2 minutes with electric mixer at medium speed. Gently stir in ¾ cup/175 mL chocolate chips. Spread evenly into prepared pan.

Bake 30 to 40 minutes or until top springs back when pressed in centre. Cool completely in pan on wire rack.

For frosting, combine powdered sugar, butter, marshmallow cream and ½ teaspoon/2.5 mL vanilla extract in medium bowl; mix until smooth. Spread frosting over top of cooled cake. Sprinkle with coconut, if desired, and ¼ cup/60 mL chocolate chips.

MAKES 16 TO 20 SERVINGS

tip

Cake can also be frosted with 2½ cups/600 mL sweetened whipped cream, whipped topping or ready-to-spread vanilla frosting. If using whipped cream or whipped topping, cover and refrigerate cake until ready to serve. Refrigerate any leftovers.

CHOCOLATE
PEANUT BUTTER
SCRUMPETS

SCRUMPETS

- 1 cup/250 mL all-purpose flour

- 1 cup/250 mL **Quaker® 100% Whole Grain Large Flake Oats or Quaker® 100% Whole Grain Quick Oats** (uncooked)

- 2 teaspoons/10 mL baking powder

- 6 tablespoons/90 mL butter or margarine, chilled and cut into pieces

- ½ cup/125 mL semi-sweet chocolate chips

- ½ cup/125 mL creamy peanut butter

- ½ cup/125 mL honey

- ½ cup/125 mL milk

- 1 egg

- 1 teaspoon/5 mL vanilla extract

GLAZE

- ¼ cup/60 mL honey

- ¼ cup/60 mL unsweetened cocoa powder

- 1 to 2 tablespoons/15 to 30 mL warm water

Heat oven to 375°F/190°C.

For scrumpets, combine flour, oats and baking powder in large bowl; mix well. Cut in butter with pastry blender or two knives until mixture resembles coarse crumbs. Stir in chocolate chips. Combine peanut butter, honey, milk, egg and vanilla extract in medium bowl using wire whisk or fork; blend well. Add to oat mixture all at once; stir with fork just until dry ingredients are moistened. (Do not overmix.)

Spray measuring tablespoon/15 mL measure with nonstick cooking spray. For each scrumpet, drop 2 heaping tablespoons/30 mL dough in mounds 2 inches apart onto ungreased cookie sheets.

Bake 12 to 14 minutes or until golden brown. Remove to wire racks; cool 5 minutes.

For glaze, combine honey, cocoa and enough water to make pourable mixture in small bowl; blend well. Drizzle over scrumpets. Serve warm or at room temperature.

MAKES 16 SCRUMPETS

CHOCOLATE-KISSED THUMBPRINT COOKIES

1   cup/250 mL (2 sticks) margarine or butter, slightly softened

1   cup/250 mL firmly packed brown sugar

2   eggs, separated

1   teaspoon/5 mL vanilla extract

2   cups/500 mL **Quaker® 100% Whole Grain Large Flake Oats** or **Quaker® 100% Whole Grain Quick Oats** (uncooked)

1⅔   cups/400 mL ground macadamia nuts or pecans, divided

1¼   cups/300 mL all-purpose flour

48   foil-wrapped milk chocolate candies or white- and chocolate-striped candies, unwrapped

Heat oven to 350°F/180°C. Lightly grease cookie sheets.

Beat margarine and brown sugar until creamy. Add egg yolks and vanilla extract; beat well. Add combined oats, ⅔ cup/150 mL ground nuts and flour; mix well.

Beat egg whites in small bowl with fork until frothy. Shape dough into 1-inch balls. Dip in egg whites; press one side into remaining 1 cup/250 mL nuts. Place balls, nut side up, 1 inch apart on prepared cookie sheets; press thumb deeply in centre of each.

Bake 8 minutes; remove from oven. Place one chocolate piece in each centre. Return to oven and continue baking 5 to 7 minutes or until cookies are lightly browned. Remove to wire racks. Cool completely. Store in tightly covered container.

MAKES 48 COOKIES

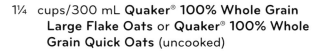

CHOCOLATE RASPBERRY
STREUSEL SQUARES

1¼ cups/300 mL **Quaker® 100% Whole Grain Large Flake Oats** or **Quaker® 100% Whole Grain Quick Oats** (uncooked)

1¼ cups/300 mL all-purpose flour

⅓ cup/75 mL granulated sugar

⅓ cup/75 mL firmly packed brown sugar

½ teaspoon/2.5 mL baking powder

¼ teaspoon/1.25 mL salt (optional)

¾ cup/175 mL (1½ sticks) margarine or butter, chilled and cut into pieces

¾ cup/175 mL raspberry preserves or jam (about 10 ounces/285 grams)

1 cup/250 mL (6 ounces/170 grams) semi-sweet chocolate chips

¼ cup/60 mL chopped almonds (optional)

½ cup/125 mL white chocolate chips, melted (optional)

Heat oven to 375°F/190°C.

Combine oats, flour, granulated sugar, brown sugar, baking powder and, if desired, salt in large bowl. Cut in margarine with pastry blender or two knives until mixture is crumbly. Reserve 1 cup/250 mL oat mixture for streusel. Press remaining mixture onto bottom of ungreased 8-inch square baking pan. Bake 10 minutes. Transfer to wire rack.

Spread preserves evenly over hot crust to within ½ inch of edges. Sprinkle evenly with chocolate chips. Combine reserved oat mixture and almonds, if desired; sprinkle over chocolate chips, patting gently.

Bake 30 to 35 minutes or until golden brown. Cool completely in pan on wire rack. Drizzle with melted white chocolate chips, if desired. Let chocolate set before cutting into squares. Store tightly covered.

MAKES 24 SQUARES

CHOCOLATE COFFEE TOFFEE OATMEAL COOKIES

¼ cup/60 mL boiling water

½ to 1 teaspoon/2.5 to 5 mL instant coffee powder

1⅓ cups/325 mL firmly packed brown sugar

1 cup/250 mL (2 sticks) 65% vegetable oil spread, softened

1 egg

1½ teaspoons/7.5 mL vanilla extract

3 cups/750 mL **Quaker® 100% Whole Grain Large Flake Oats** or **Quaker® 100% Whole Grain Quick Oats** (uncooked)

1¼ cups/300 mL all-purpose flour*

¾ teaspoon/3.75 mL salt

½ teaspoon/2.5 mL baking soda

1 package (8 ounces/225 grams) milk chocolate toffee bits (about 1⅓ cups/325 mL)

1½ cups/350 mL semi-sweet chocolate chips

1 cup/250 mL coarsely crumbled sugar cones (about 5 cones)

*If using large flake oats, add 2 tablespoons/30 mL additional flour.

Heat oven to 350°F/180°C. Line cookie sheets with parchment paper or nonstick aluminum foil, or use nonstick cookie sheets.

Dissolve coffee in boiling water; cool to room temperature. Beat brown sugar and spread in large bowl with electric mixer at medium speed until creamy. Add egg; beat well. Beat in coffee and vanilla extract. Combine oats, flour, salt and baking soda in medium bowl; mix well. Gradually add to creamed mixture, beating well after each addition. Stir in toffee bits, chocolate chips and sugar cones. Drop dough by heaping measuring tablespoonfuls/15 mL in mounds 2 inches apart onto prepared cookie sheets.

Bake 12 to 14 minutes, just until golden brown. Cool 1 minute on cookie sheets; remove to wire racks. Cool completely. Store loosely covered.

MAKES ABOUT 60 COOKIES

2 cups/500 mL (12-ounce/360-gram package) semi-sweet chocolate chips, divided

1¼ cups/300 mL all-purpose flour

2 teaspoons/10 mL baking powder

¼ teaspoon/1.25 mL baking soda

¼ teaspoon/1.25 mL salt (optional)

1 cup/250 mL (2 sticks) margarine or butter, softened

¾ cup/175 mL firmly packed brown sugar

1 egg

1 teaspoon/5 mL vanilla extract

2 cups/500 mL **Quaker® 100% Whole Grain Large Flake Oats or Quaker® 100% Whole Grain Quick Oats** (uncooked)

Heat oven to 350°F/180°C.

Melt 1 cup/250 mL chocolate chips in small saucepan over low heat; cool.

Combine flour, baking powder, baking soda and, if desired, salt in medium bowl; mix well. Beat margarine and brown sugar in large bowl with electric mixer until creamy. Blend in melted chocolate, egg and vanilla extract. Gradually add flour mixture; mix well. Stir in oats and remaining 1 cup/250 mL chocolate chips. Drop by rounded tablespoonfuls/15 mL onto ungreased cookie sheets.

Bake 12 to 14 minutes or until set. Cool 2 minutes on cookie sheets; remove to wire racks. Store tightly covered.

MAKES 42 COOKIES

DOUBLE-CHOCOLATE BAR COOKIES: Heat oven to 375°F/190°C. Press dough evenly onto bottom of greased 13×9-inch baking pan. Bake about 25 minutes or until wooden pick inserted in centre comes out clean. Cool completely in pan. Cut into bars. Store tightly covered. Makes 32 bars.

CHOCOLATE
CHIP SNACKIN'
CAKE

TOPPING

¼ cup/60 mL all-purpose flour

¼ cup/60 mL firmly packed brown sugar

3 tablespoons/45 mL chilled butter, cut into pieces

½ cup/125 mL **Quaker® 100% Whole Grain Large Flake Oats or Quaker® 100% Whole Grain Quick Oats** (uncooked)

¼ cup/60 mL mini chocolate chips

CAKE

1 cup/250 mL boiling water

½ cup/125 mL **Quaker® 100% Whole Grain Large Flake Oats** or **Quaker® 100% Whole Grain Quick Oats** (uncooked)

1¾ cups/450 mL all-purpose flour

1 teaspoon/5 mL baking soda

¼ teaspoon/1.25 mL salt

¾ cup/175 mL granulated sugar

¾ cup/175 mL firmly packed brown sugar

⅓ cup/75 mL canola oil

1 egg

1½ teaspoons/7.5 mL vanilla extract

¼ cup/60 mL mini chocolate chips

Heat oven to 350°F/180°C. Lightly spray 8- or 9-inch square metal baking pan with nonstick cooking spray.

For topping, combine ¼ cup/60 mL flour and ¼ cup/60 mL brown sugar in small bowl; mix well. Cut in butter with pastry blender or two knives until mixture is crumbly. Stir in ½ cup/125 mL oats and ¼ cup/60 mL chocolate chips.

For cake, combine boiling water and ½ cup/125 mL oats in small bowl. Set aside. Combine 1¾ cups/450 mL flour, baking soda and salt in medium bowl; mix well.

Beat granulated sugar, brown sugar and oil in large bowl with electric mixer until well blended. Add egg and vanilla extract; beat well. Add flour mixture and oat mixture; mix just until dry ingredients are moistened. (Do not overmix.) Stir in ¼ cup/60 mL chocolate chips. Pour batter into pan. Sprinkle with reserved topping.

Bake 50 to 60 minutes or until wooden pick inserted in centre comes out with a few moist crumbs clinging to it. Cool in pan on wire rack. Store tightly covered at room temperature.

MAKES 16 SERVINGS

MARBLED
CHOCOLATE CHIP
OATMEAL COOKIES

2   cups/500 mL (4 sticks) butter or margarine, softened

2   cups/500 mL granulated sugar

1   cup/250 mL firmly packed brown sugar

4   eggs

1   tablespoon/15 mL vanilla extract

4¼ cups/1 litre plus 60 mL all-purpose flour, divided

2   teaspoons/10 mL baking soda

1   teaspoon/5 mL salt (optional)

½   cup/125 mL unsweetened cocoa powder

2   cups/500 mL **Quaker® 100% Whole Grain Large Flake Oats** or **Quaker® 100% Whole Grain Quick Oats** (uncooked), divided

2   cups/500 mL (12-ounce/360-gram package) **semi-sweet** chocolate chips, divided

Beat butter, granulated sugar and brown sugar in large bowl until creamy. Add eggs and vanilla extract; beat well. Add combined 4 cups/1 litre flour, baking soda and, if desired, salt; mix well.

Divide dough evenly between two bowls. Add cocoa to one bowl and add remaining ¼ cup/60 mL flour to second bowl; mix well. Add 1 cup/250 ml oats and 1 cup/250 ml chocolate chips to each bowl; mix well. Cover and chill both doughs 2 hours.

Heat oven to 375°F/190°C. To shape cookies, remove small portion of each dough; keep remainder refrigerated. Combine 1 tablespoon/15 mL of each dough, twisting doughs together to form a single cookie. Place 2 inches apart on ungreased cookie sheets. Repeat with remaining doughs.

Bake 10 to 11 minutes or until light-coloured dough is golden brown. Cool 2 minutes on cookie sheets; remove to wire racks. Cool completely. Store tightly covered.

MAKES 48 COOKIES

CHEWY COCOA COOKIES

½ cup/125 mL granulated sugar

½ cup/125 mL firmly packed brown sugar

⅓ cup/75 mL margarine

2 large egg whites or 1 egg

½ cup/125 mL fat-free (skim) milk

1 teaspoon/5 mL vanilla extract

2 cups/500 mL **Quaker® 100% Whole Grain Large Flake Oats** or **Quaker® 100% Whole Grain Quick Oats** (uncooked)

1 cup/250 mL all-purpose flour

⅓ cup/75 mL unsweetened cocoa powder

1½ teaspoons/7.5 mL baking powder

1 cup/250 mL raisins

Heat oven to 350°F/180°C. Lightly spray cookie sheet with nonstick cooking spray.

Beat granulated sugar, brown sugar, margarine and egg whites in large bowl until creamy. Add milk and vanilla extract; beat well. Combine oats, flour, cocoa and baking powder in separate bowl; mix well. Add to creamed mixture; mix well. Stir in raisins.

Bake 10 to 12 minutes or just until set. Cool 1 minute on cookie sheet; remove to wire rack. Cool completely. Store tightly covered.

MAKES 30 COOKIES

COLOSSAL BROWNIE
ICE CREAM
SANDWICH

TOPPING

- ⅓ cup/75 mL **Quaker® 100% Whole Grain Large Flake Oats** or **Quaker® 100% Whole Grain Quick Oats** (uncooked)

- 3 tablespoons/45 mL all-purpose flour

- 2 tablespoons/30 mL firmly packed brown sugar

- ⅓ cup/75 mL peanut butter (not reduced fat)

- 1 tablespoon/15 mL margarine or butter

BROWNIES

- 1 cup/250 mL (6 ounces/ 170 grams) semi-sweet chocolate chips

- ½ cup/125 mL (1 stick) margarine or butter

- ¾ cup/175 mL granulated sugar

- 1 teaspoon/5 mL vanilla extract

- 2 eggs

- 1 cup/250 mL all-purpose flour

- ¾ cup/175 mL **Quaker® 100% Whole Grain Large Flake Oats** or **Quaker® 100% Whole Grain Quick Oats** (uncooked)

- ½ teaspoon/2.5 mL baking powder

- ¼ teaspoon/1.25 mL salt (optional)

- 1 quart/1 litre fat-free or low fat vanilla ice cream or frozen yogurt, slightly softened

Heat oven to 350°F/180°C. Line two 8- or 9-inch round cake pans with aluminum foil, allowing foil to extend over sides of pans. Spray with nonstick cooking spray.

For topping, combine ⅓ cup/75 mL oats, 3 tablespoons/45 mL flour and brown sugar in large bowl. Cut in peanut butter and 1 tablespoon/15 mL margarine with pastry blender or two knives until mixture is crumbly. Set aside.

For brownies, melt chocolate chips and ½ cup/125 mL margarine in medium saucepan over low heat, stirring frequently. Remove from heat; cool slightly. Stir in granulated sugar and vanilla extract. Add eggs; mix well. Add combined 1 cup/250 mL flour, ¾ cup/175 mL oats, baking powder and, if desired, salt; mix well. Divide batter evenly between pans. Sprinkle with reserved topping, patting gently.

Bake 22 to 24 minutes for 8-inch pans (20 to 22 minutes for 9-inch pans) or just until centre of brownie is set. (Do not overbake.) Cool completely in pans on wire rack.

Spread softened ice cream evenly over one brownie while still in pan. Lift second brownie out of pan; remove foil. With topping side up, place brownie on top of ice cream, pressing gently. Cover and freeze several hours or overnight. Remove from freezer 10 to 15 minutes before cutting. Lift from pan using foil edges. Remove foil; cut into wedges. Individually wrap wedges and store in freezer.

MAKES 12 SERVINGS

NO-BAKE
COCOA OATMEAL
TREATS

2 cups/500 mL granulated sugar

½ cup/125 mL (1 stick) butter or margarine

½ cup/125 mL milk

⅓ cup/75 mL unsweetened cocoa powder

2½ cups/600 mL **Quaker® 100% Whole Grain Large Flake Oats** or **Quaker® 100% Whole Grain Quick Oats** (uncooked)

⅓ cup/75 mL peanut butter

½ cup/125 mL chopped unsalted peanuts (optional)

2 teaspoons/10 mL vanilla extract

Line three cookie sheets with waxed paper or aluminum foil.

Combine sugar, butter, milk and cocoa in medium saucepan. Cook over medium heat, stirring constantly, until mixture comes to a rolling boil. Continue to boil 1 minute, stirring constantly. Remove from heat. Add oats, peanut butter, peanuts, if desired, and vanilla extract; mix well.

Drop by heaping teaspoons/5 mL onto prepared cookie sheets; cool completely. Store on plate covered with foil or plastic wrap in a cool dry place.

MAKES 48 TREATS

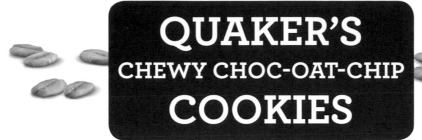
1 cup/250 mL (2 sticks) margarine or butter, softened

1 cup/250 mL firmly packed brown sugar

½ cup/125 mL granulated sugar

2 eggs

2 tablespoons/30 mL milk

2 teaspoons/10 mL vanilla extract

1¾ cups/450 mL all-purpose flour

1 teaspoon/5 mL baking soda

½ teaspoon/2.5 mL salt (optional)

2½ cups/600 mL **Quaker® 100% Whole Grain Large Flake Oats or Quaker® 100% Whole Grain Quick Oats** (uncooked)

2 cups/500 mL (12 ounces/360 grams) semi-sweet chocolate chips

1 cup/250 mL chopped nuts (optional)

Heat oven to 375°F/190°C.

Beat margarine, brown sugar and granulated sugar in large bowl until creamy. Add eggs, milk and vanilla extract; beat well. Add combined flour, baking soda and, if desired, salt; mix well. Add oats, chocolate chips and, if desired, nuts; mix well. Drop dough by rounded tablespoonfuls/15 mL onto ungreased cookie sheets.

Bake 9 to 10 minutes for chewy cookies or 12 to 13 minutes for crisp cookies. Cool 1 minute on cookie sheets; remove to wire racks. Cool completely. Store tightly covered.

MAKES ABOUT 60 COOKIES

BAR COOKIES: Press dough onto bottom of ungreased 13×9-inch baking pan. Bake 30 to 35 minutes or until light golden brown. Cool completely in pan on wire rack. Cut into bars. Store tightly covered. Makes 32 bars.

tip

Substitute 1 cup/250 mL butterscotch chips or peanut butter and milk chocolate chips or candy-coated chocolate pieces for chocolate chips.

CHOCO
PEANUT BUTTER
BARS

1 cup/250 mL firmly packed brown sugar

½ cup/125 mL (1 stick) butter or margarine, softened

½ cup/125 mL peanut butter

1 egg

1 teaspoon/5 mL vanilla extract

1 cup/250 mL all-purpose flour

½ teaspoon/2.5 mL baking soda

1½ cups/350 mL **Quaker® 100% Whole Grain Large Flake Oats** or **Quaker® 100% Whole Grain Quick Oats** (uncooked)

1 cup/250 mL (6 ounces/170 grams) semi-sweet chocolate chips

Heat oven to 350°F/180°C.

Beat brown sugar, butter and peanut butter in medium bowl until creamy. Add egg and vanilla extract; beat well. Add flour and baking soda; mix well. Stir in oats and chocolate chips. Spread into ungreased 13×9-inch baking pan.

Bake 20 to 25 minutes or until golden brown and edges pull away from sides of pan. Cool completely. Cut into bars.

MAKES 24 BARS

CHOCOLATE-HAZELNUT
OATMEAL
REFRIGERATOR COOKIES

2 cups/500 mL granulated sugar

6 tablespoons/90 mL unsweetened cocoa powder

½ cup/125 mL (1 stick) 65% vegetable oil spread

½ cup/125 mL whole milk

3 cups/750 mL **Quaker® 100% Whole Grain Large Flake Oats** or **Quaker® 100% Whole Grain Quick Oats** (uncooked)

1 cup/250 mL chopped hazelnuts

⅔ cup/150 mL chocolate-hazelnut spread

1 teaspoon/5 mL vanilla extract

Line three cookie sheets with waxed paper.

Combine sugar, cocoa, spread and milk in large saucepan. Cook and stir over medium heat until mixture comes to a full boil. Continue boiling 1 minute without stirring. Remove pan from heat. Immediately add oats, hazelnuts, chocolate-hazelnut spread and vanilla extract; mix well.

Working quickly, drop mixture by rounded measuring tablespoonfuls/15 mL onto prepared cookie sheets. Refrigerate until well chilled. Transfer to airtight containers, separating layers with waxed paper. Store in refrigerator.

MAKES 72 COOKIES

SNACKS
AND BARS

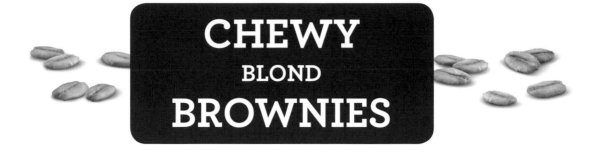

CHEWY BLOND BROWNIES

⅔ cup/150 mL (1⅓ sticks) margarine or butter, softened

1¼ cups/300 mL firmly packed brown sugar

1⅓ cups/325 mL **Quaker® 100% Whole Grain Large Flake Oats** or **Quaker® 100% Whole Grain Quick Oats** (uncooked)

1⅓ cups/325 mL all-purpose flour

2 eggs

½ cup/125 mL semi-sweet chocolate chips

½ cup/125 mL chopped nuts

2 teaspoons/10 mL vanilla extract

¾ teaspoon/3.75 mL baking soda

½ teaspoon/2.5 mL salt (optional)

Heat oven to 350°F/180°C. Grease 13×9-inch baking pan.

Beat margarine and brown sugar in large bowl until fluffy. Add oats, flour, egg, chocolate chips, nuts, vanilla extract, baking soda and, if desired, salt; mix well. Spread into prepared pan.

Bake 25 to 30 minutes or until golden brown. Cool completely. Cut into bars.

MAKES 32 BARS

VARIATION: For iced brownies, sprinkle 2 cups/500 mL chocolate chips over brownies immediately after baking. Let stand 10 minutes; spread melted chocolate chips evenly with spatula. Cool completely before cutting.

WINTER TRAIL MIX

2 cups/500 mL **Quaker® 100% Whole Grain Large Flake Oats** (uncooked)

1½ cups/350 mL **Quaker® Oatmeal Squares™ Cereal**

¼ cup/60 mL maple-flavoured syrup, regular or light

1 tablespoon/15 mL vegetable oil

1 teaspoon/5 mL vanilla extract

½ cup/125 mL snipped dried apple chunks

½ cup/125 mL snipped dried apricots

½ cup/125 mL dried cranberries

¾ cup/175 mL lightly salted almonds or dry-roasted peanuts

Heat oven to 325°F/160°C. Combine oats and cereal in large bowl. Combine maple syrup, oil and vanilla extract in small bowl; pour over cereal mixture. Mix until well coated. Transfer to 15×10-inch jelly-roll pan.

Bake 20 to 25 minutes until oats are golden brown, stirring every 10 minutes.

Remove from oven. Immediately stir in apples, apricots, cranberries and nuts. Cool completely in pan on wire rack. Store loosely covered up to 1 week.

MAKES 12 SERVINGS

SERVING SUGGESTIONS:

• Spread a whole grain bagel half with peanut butter; sprinkle with trail mix, pressing lightly into peanut butter.
• Mix trail mix with light cream cheese; spread on whole grain bagels or whole wheat toast.
• Stir trail mix into low fat vanilla yogurt or low fat cottage cheese for breakfast or a snack.
• Make a crunchy breakfast parfait by layering trail mix with fresh fruit (sliced bananas, chopped apples, grape halves, pineapple chunks) and low fat yogurt.
• Serve cold with milk.
• Stir trail mix into pancake batter before cooking.
• Put individual servings of trail mix in resealable plastic bags to eat away from home.

TRIPLE PEANUT BUTTER
OATMEAL
BARS

1½ cups/350 mL firmly packed brown sugar

1 cup/250 mL peanut butter

½ cup/125 mL (1 stick) margarine or butter, softened

2 large eggs

1 teaspoon/5 mL vanilla extract

2 cups/500 mL **Quaker® 100% Whole Grain Large Flake Oats** or **Quaker® 100% Whole Grain Quick Oats** (uncooked)

1 cup/250 mL all-purpose flour

½ teaspoon/2.5 mL baking soda

1 bag (8 ounces/225 grams) candy-coated peanut butter pieces

½ cup/125 mL chopped peanuts

Heat oven to 350°F/180°C. Lightly spray 13×9-inch baking pan with nonstick cooking spray.

Beat brown sugar, peanut butter and margarine in large bowl with electric mixer until creamy. Add eggs and vanilla extract; beat well. Add combined oats, flour and baking soda; mix well. Stir in peanut butter pieces. Spread dough evenly into pan. Sprinkle with peanuts, pressing in lightly with fingers.

Bake 35 to 40 minutes or just until centre is set. Cool completely on wire rack. Cut into bars. Store tightly covered.

MAKES 32 BARS

CHEWY OATMEAL SPICE BARS

¾ cup/175 mL firmly packed brown sugar

½ cup/125 mL granulated sugar

¼ cup/60 mL (½ stick) margarine

¾ cup/175 mL apple butter or applesauce

2 egg whites or 1 egg

2 tablespoons/30 mL fat-free (skim) milk

2 teaspoons/10 mL vanilla extract

1½ cups/350 mL all-purpose flour

1 teaspoon/5 mL baking soda

1 teaspoon/5 mL ground cinnamon

½ teaspoon/2.5 mL salt (optional)

¼ teaspoon/1.25 mL ground nutmeg (optional)

3 cups/750 mL **Quaker® 100% Whole Grain Large Flake Oats** or **Quaker® 100% Whole Grain Quick Oats** (uncooked)

1 cup/250 mL raisins or diced dried mixed fruit

Heat oven to 350°F/180°C. Lightly spray 13×9-inch baking pan with nonstick cooking spray.

Beat brown sugar, granulated sugar and margarine in large bowl until well blended. Add apple butter, egg whites, milk and vanilla extract; beat well. Add combined flour, baking soda, cinnamon, and, if desired, salt and nutmeg; mix well. Stir in oats and raisins; mix well. (Dough will be moist.) Press dough evenly onto bottom of baking pan.

Bake 30 to 35 minutes or until light golden brown. Cool completely in pan. Store in tightly covered container.

MAKES 32 BARS

DOUBLE CRUNCH
GRANOLA
BARS

4   cups/1 litre **Quaker® 100% Whole Grain Quick Oats** or
    4½ cups/1.125 litres **Quaker® 100% Whole Grain Large Flake
    Oats** (uncooked)

1½ cups/350 mL chopped nuts

1   cup/250 mL firmly packed brown sugar

¾   cup/175 mL (1½ sticks) butter or margarine, melted

½   cup/125 mL honey or corn syrup

1   teaspoon/5 mL vanilla extract

½   teaspoon/2.5 mL salt (optional)

Heat oven to 350°F/180°C. Generously grease 15×10-inch jelly-roll pan.

Combine all ingredients; mix well. Press firmly into prepared pan.

Bake 10 to 12 minutes or until golden brown and bubbly. Cool completely in pan on wire rack. Cut into bars.

MAKES 32 BARS

TERRIFIC TRAIL MIX

3 cups/750 mL **Quaker® Oatmeal Squares™ Cereal**

1½ cups/350 mL **Quaker® 100% Whole Grain Large Flake Oats** or **Quaker® 100% Whole Grain Quick Oats** (uncooked)

⅓ cup/75 mL roasted salted soy nuts or dry-roasted peanuts

¼ cup/60 mL honey

2 tablespoons/30 mL vegetable oil

1 cup/250 mL mixed dried fruit bits

½ cup/125 mL mini candy-coated milk chocolate candies

Heat oven to 350°F/180°C. Spray 15×10-inch jelly-roll pan with nonstick cooking spray.

Combine cereal, oats and soy nuts in large bowl. Combine honey and oil in small bowl; mix well. Add to cereal mixture; mix well. Spread mixture in single layer on prepared pan.

Bake 12 to 15 minutes, stirring three times during baking. Remove from oven; stir to loosen mix from pan. Cool completely in pan on wire rack. Stir in dried fruit and candy. Store tightly covered.

MAKES ABOUT 7 CUPS/1.75 LITRES

CAPPUCCINO
CARAMEL OAT
BARS

BARS

3 cups/750 mL **Quaker®
100% Whole Grain Large
Flake Oats** or **Quaker®
100% Whole Grain Quick
Oats** (uncooked)

2⅓ cups/575 mL all-purpose
flour

1½ cups/350 mL chopped pecans,
divided

1 teaspoon/5 mL baking soda

¼ teaspoon/1.25 mL salt

2 cups/500 mL firmly packed
brown sugar

1 cup/250 mL (2 sticks) butter
or margarine, softened

2 large eggs

1 tablespoon/15 mL instant
coffee powder or instant
espresso coffee

2 teaspoons/10 mL vanilla
extract

¾ cup/175 mL spoonable caramel
ice cream topping

GLAZE

2 tablespoons/30 mL very hot milk

1 teaspoon/5 mL instant coffee powder or instant espresso coffee

1 cup/250 mL powdered sugar

Heat oven to 350°F/180°C. Lightly grease 15×10-inch jelly-roll pan.

For bars, combine oats, flour, 1 cup/250 mL pecans, baking soda and salt in large bowl; mix well. Beat brown sugar and butter in large bowl with electric mixer until creamy. Combine eggs, 1 tablespoon/15 mL coffee powder and vanilla extract in small bowl; mix until well blended. Add to creamed mixture; continue beating until light and fluffy. Stir in oat mixture; mix well. (Dough will be very thick.) Reserve 2 cups/500 mL dough for topping. Using lightly floured hands, press remaining dough evenly onto bottom of prepared pan. Spread caramel topping evenly over crust to within ¼ inch of edges. Drop spoonfuls of reserved dough over caramel topping; sprinkle with remaining ½ cup/125 mL pecans.

Bake 20 to 25 minutes or until centre feels firm when lightly touched. (Do not overbake.) Cool completely in pan on wire rack.

For glaze, combine milk and 1 teaspoon/5 mL coffee powder in small bowl; stir until coffee powder dissolves. Add powdered sugar; stir until smooth. Drizzle over cookies in pan. Let stand 15 minutes to set glaze. Cut into bars. Store tightly covered.

MAKES 48 BARS

tip

*Instant coffee granules or
freeze-dried coffee are not
recommended for this recipe.
Fat-free caramel ice cream topping
is not recommended for this
recipe. If ice cream topping is very
thick, microwave on HIGH 10 to
20 seconds or until spreadable.*

BERRY BERRY STREUSEL BARS

CRUST

1½ cups/350 mL **Quaker® 100% Whole Grain Large Flake Oats** or **Quaker® 100% Whole Grain Quick Oats** (uncooked)

1¼ cups/300 mL all-purpose flour

½ cup/125 mL firmly packed brown sugar

¾ cup/175 mL (1½ sticks) margarine or butter, melted

FILLING

1 cup/250 mL fresh or frozen blueberries (do not thaw)

⅓ cup/75 mL raspberry or strawberry preserves

1 teaspoon/5 mL all-purpose flour

½ teaspoon/2.5 mL grated lemon peel (optional)

Heat oven to 350°F/180°C.

For crust, combine oats, 1¼ cups/300 mL flour, brown sugar and margarine in large bowl; mix until crumbly. Reserve 1 cup oat mixture for topping. Press remaining oat mixture evenly onto bottom of ungreased 8- or 9-inch square baking pan.

Bake 13 to 15 minutes or until light golden brown. Cool slightly on wire rack.

For filling, combine blueberries, preserves, 1 teaspoon/ 5 mL flour and lemon peel, if desired, in medium bowl; mix gently. Spread evenly over crust to within ½ inch of edges. Sprinkle with reserved oat mixture, patting gently.

Bake 20 to 22 minutes or until light golden brown. Cool completely in pan on wire rack. Cut into bars. Store tightly covered.

MAKES 16 BARS

MAPLE PECAN OATMEAL BARS

BARS

¾ cup/175 mL (1½ sticks) margarine or butter

2¼ cups/550 mL **Quaker® 100% Whole Grain Large Flake Oats** or **Quaker® 100% Whole Grain Quick Oats** (uncooked)

2 cups/500 mL all-purpose flour

1½ cups/350 mL firmly packed brown sugar

¾ cup/175 mL shredded coconut (optional)

1 teaspoon/5 mL baking soda

1 teaspoon/5 mL salt (optional)

⅓ cup/75 mL **Aunt Jemima® Original Syrup**

1 egg, lightly beaten

1 teaspoon/5 mL vanilla extract

TOPPING

1½ cups/350 mL chopped pecans (about 6 ounces/170 grams)

¼ cup/60 mL firmly packed brown sugar

⅓ cup/75 mL **Aunt Jemima® Original Syrup**

Heat oven to 350°F/180°C. Lightly spray 13×9-inch baking pan with nonstick cooking spray. Melt margarine. Set aside to cool.

Combine oats, flour, 1½ cups/350 mL brown sugar, coconut, if desired, baking soda and, if desired, salt in large bowl; mix well. (Dough will be stiff.) Combine melted margarine, ⅓ cup/75 mL syrup, egg and vanilla extract in small bowl; mix well. Add to oat mixture; mix well. Press dough evenly onto bottom of pan.

For topping, combine pecans and ¼ cup/60 mL brown sugar in small bowl. Sprinkle evenly over dough; press down lightly. Drizzle ⅓ cup/75 mL syrup evenly over pecans.

Bake 35 to 38 minutes or until edges are set but middle is soft. Cool completely in pan on wire rack. Cut into bars. Store tightly covered.

MAKES 32 BARS

CHEWY
FRUIT AND OATMEAL
BARS

¾ cup/175 mL firmly packed brown sugar

½ cup/125 mL granulated sugar

1 container (8 ounces/225 grams) low fat vanilla or plain yogurt

2 egg whites, lightly beaten

2 tablespoons/30 mL vegetable oil

2 tablespoons/30 mL fat-free (skim) milk

2 teaspoons/10 mL vanilla extract

1½ cups/350 mL all-purpose flour

1 teaspoon/5 mL baking soda

1 teaspoon/5 mL ground cinnamon

½ teaspoon/2.5 mL salt (optional)

3 cups/750 mL **Quaker® 100% Whole Grain Large Flake Oats** or **Quaker® 100% Whole Grain Quick Oats** (uncooked)

1 cup/250 mL diced dried mixed fruit, raisins or dried cranberries

Heat oven to 350°F/180°C.

Combine brown sugar, granulated sugar, yogurt, egg whites, oil, milk and vanilla extract in large bowl; mix well. Combine flour, baking soda, cinnamon and, if desired, salt in medium bowl; mix well. Add to yogurt mixture; mix well. Stir in oats and fruit. Spread dough onto bottom of ungreased 13×9-inch baking pan.

Bake 28 to 32 minutes or until light golden brown. Cool completely on wire rack. Cut into bars. Store tightly covered.

MAKES 24 BARS

CRANBERRY
PISTACHIO
OAT BARS

1 cup/250 mL (2 sticks) 65% vegetable oil spread

½ cup/125 mL firmly packed brown sugar

1 package (17.4 ounces/493 grams) cinnamon swirl quick bread and coffee cake mix, divided

¼ cup/60 mL **Tropicana Pure Premium**® orange juice or **Dole**® 100% orange juice

1 egg

1 teaspoon/5 mL vanilla extract

1½ cups/350 mL **Quaker**® **100% Whole Grain Large Flake Oats** or **Quaker**® **100% Whole Grain Quick Oats** (uncooked)

½ cup/125 mL coarsely chopped pistachios

½ to ¾ cup/125 to 175 mL dried cranberries

Heat oven to 375°F/190°C. Spray 13×9-inch metal baking pan with nonstick cooking spray.

Beat spread and brown sugar in large bowl with electric mixer at medium speed until creamy. Add quick bread mix and clear packet of cinnamon swirl (reserve foil glaze packet for later use), orange juice, egg and vanilla extract. Beat just until blended. Add oats, pistachios and cranberries. Mix at low speed just until combined. Spread evenly into prepared pan.

Bake 30 to 34 minutes or until edges are golden brown and wooden pick inserted in centre comes out with a few moist crumbs clinging to it. Cool completely in pan on wire rack.

Squeeze reserved foil packet from mix about 10 times. Cut tip off one corner of packet; squeeze glaze decoratively over bars in pan. Cut into bars.

MAKES 24 BARS

Walnuts or pecans may be substituted for pistachios.

HARVEST FRUIT BARS

1 package (6 ounces/170 grams) diced dried mixed fruit bits

1 cup/250 mL chopped banana (about 2 medium)

⅔ cup/150 mL **Tropicana Pure Premium**® orange juice or **Dole**® 100% orange juice*

1½ teaspoons/7.5 mL apple pie spice or ground cinnamon, divided

1¾ cups/450 mL whole wheat flour or all-purpose flour

1½ cups/350 mL **Quaker**® 100% Whole Grain Large Flake Oats or **Quaker**® 100% Whole Grain Quick Oats (uncooked)

1 cup/250 mL (2 sticks) margarine or butter, softened

1 cup/250 mL firmly packed brown sugar

½ cup/125 mL chopped nuts

If using large flake oats, decrease orange juice to ½ cup/125 mL.

Heat oven to 375°F/190°C. Combine dried fruit, banana, orange juice and 1 teaspoon/5 mL apple pie spice in medium bowl. Set aside.

Combine flour, oats and remaining ½ teaspoon/2.5 mL apple pie spice in medium bowl; mix well. Beat margarine and brown sugar in large bowl with electric mixer until creamy. Add oat mixture; beat until crumbly. Reserve ¾ cup/175 mL mixture for topping. Press remaining oat mixture onto bottom of ungreased 13×9-inch baking pan. Bake 13 to 15 minutes or until light golden brown.

Spread fruit mixture evenly over crust to within ¼ inch of edges. Add nuts to reserved topping mixture; mix well. Sprinkle evenly over fruit; pat down lightly.

Bake 16 to 20 minutes or until golden brown. Cool completely. Cut into bars. Store loosely covered.

MAKES 32 BARS

PEANUT
BUTTER 'N' FUDGE
FILLED BARS

- 2 cups/500 mL firmly packed brown sugar
- 1 cup/250 mL (2 sticks) butter or margarine, softened
- ¼ cup plus 2 tablespoons/90 mL peanut butter, divided
- 2 eggs
- 2 cups/500 mL all-purpose flour
- 1 teaspoon/5 mL baking soda
- ¼ teaspoon/1.25 mL salt (optional)
- 2 cups/500 mL **Quaker® 100% Whole Grain Large Flake Oats** or **Quaker® 100% Whole Grain Quick Oats** (uncooked)
- 1 can (14 ounces/398 grams) sweetened condensed milk (not evaporated milk)
- 2 cups/500 mL (12-ounce/360-gram package) semi-sweet chocolate chips
- ⅔ cup/150 mL chopped dry-roasted peanuts

Heat oven to 350°F/180°C.

Beat brown sugar, butter and ¼ cup/60 mL peanut butter in large bowl with electric mixer until light and fluffy. Beat in eggs. Add combined flour, baking soda and, if desired, salt; beat well. Stir in oats; mix well. Reserve 1 cup/ 250 mL oat mixture. Spread remaining oat mixture evenly onto bottom of ungreased 13×9-inch baking pan.

Combine condensed milk, chocolate chips and remaining 2 tablespoons/ 30 mL peanut butter in small saucepan. Cook over low heat until chocolate is melted, stirring constantly. Remove from heat; stir in peanuts. Spread mixture evenly over crust. Drop remaining oat mixture by teaspoonfuls evenly over chocolate mixture.

Bake 25 to 30 minutes or until light golden brown. Cool completely on wire rack. Cut into bars.

MAKES 32 BARS

SPIRITED SOUTHERN SWEET POTATO BARS

2 cups/500 mL **Quaker® 100% Whole Grain Large Flake Oats** or **Quaker® 100% Whole Grain Quick Oats** (uncooked)

1½ cups/350 mL all-purpose flour

¼ teaspoon/1.25 mL salt (optional)

⅛ to ¼ teaspoon/0.625 to 1.25 mL ground red pepper

1 cup/250 mL (2 sticks) butter or margarine, softened

⅔ cup/150 mL granulated sugar

1 teaspoon/5 mL vanilla extract

2 cups/500 mL mashed cooked sweet potatoes or canned pumpkin

2 eggs, lightly beaten

¾ cup/175 mL firmly packed brown sugar

2 tablespoons/30 mL bourbon or ½ teaspoon/2.5 mL rum extract

1 cup/250 mL chopped pecans

Heat oven to 375°F/190°C. Lightly grease 13×9-inch baking pan.

Combine oats and flour in large bowl; mix well. Measure ⅔ cup/150 mL of mixture into small bowl; stir in salt, if desired, and red pepper. Set aside.

Add butter, granulated sugar and vanilla extract to remaining oat mixture; blend with electric mixer at low to medium speed until crumbly. Reserve 1 cup/250 mL for topping. Press remaining mixture evenly onto bottom of prepared pan. Bake 15 minutes; remove pan from oven.

Combine sweet potatoes, reserved ⅔ cup/150 mL oat mixture, eggs, brown sugar and bourbon in separate bowl; mix well. Spread filling over warm crust. Add pecans to reserved topping mixture; mix well. Sprinkle evenly over sweet potato filling.

Bake 30 to 35 minutes or until topping is light golden brown. Cool in pan on wire rack. Cut into bars. Serve at room temperature. Store in refrigerator tightly covered.

MAKES 32 BARS

OATMEAL
CARAMEL WHITE CHIP
BARS

CRUST

2	cups/500 mL	all-purpose flour
1½	cups/350 mL	firmly packed brown sugar
1¼	cups/300 mL	(2½ sticks) butter or margarine, softened
1	teaspoon/5 mL	baking soda
½	teaspoon/2.5 mL	salt
2	cups/500 mL	**Quaker® 100% Whole Grain Quick Oats** (uncooked)

FILLING

2	cups/500 mL	(12-ounce/360-gram package) white chocolate chips
½	cup/125 mL	chopped nuts
1	cup/250 mL	caramel or butterscotch caramel fudge topping
3	tablespoons/45 mL	all-purpose flour

Heat oven to 350°F/180°C. Grease 13×9-inch metal baking pan.

For crust, beat 2 cups/500 mL flour, brown sugar, butter, baking soda and salt in large bowl with electric mixer until crumbly. Beat in oats at low speed just until combined. Press half of mixture (about 2½ cups/600 mL) into bottom of baking pan.

Bake 10 minutes. Cool in pan for 2 minutes.

For filling, sprinkle chips and nuts over crust. Blend caramel topping with 3 tablespoons/45 mL flour. Drizzle over chips and nuts. Crumble remaining oat mixture over chips and nuts.

Bake 18 to 22 minutes or until golden brown. Cool completely in pan on wire rack. Cut into bars.

MAKES ABOUT 36 BARS

OATMEAL
SQUARES
SNACKER-JAX

1 box (16 ounces/454 grams) **Quaker® Oatmeal Squares™ Cereal**
 (regular or cinnamon flavour)

1½ cups/350 mL roasted Spanish peanuts

½ cup/125 mL (1 stick) margarine or butter

1 cup/250 mL firmly packed brown sugar

2 tablespoons/30 mL dark corn syrup

2 tablespoons/30 mL molasses

1 teaspoon/5 mL salt (optional)

1 teaspoon/5 mL vanilla extract

1 teaspoon/5 mL baking soda

Heat oven to 250°F/120°C. Line two cookie sheets with waxed paper. Combine cereal and peanuts in 13×9-inch baking pan.

Melt margarine in small saucepan over medium heat. Stir in brown sugar, corn syrup, molasses and, if desired, salt. Bring to a boil. Stir well. Boil 2 minutes without stirring. Remove from heat. Add vanilla extract and baking soda; mix well. Immediately pour over cereal mixture; stir with wooden spoon to evenly coat all pieces with syrup mixture.

Bake 1 hour, stirring every 20 minutes. Transfer to prepared cookie sheets, spreading mixture into even layer. Cool completely. Break into bite-size pieces. Store tightly covered at room temperature.

MAKES 10 CUPS/2.5 LITRES

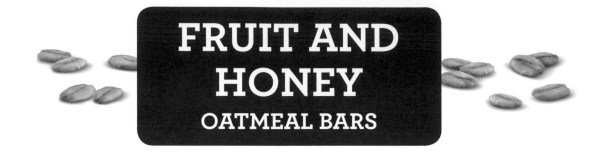

FRUIT AND HONEY
OATMEAL BARS

¼ cup/60 mL honey

¼ cup/60 mL (½ stick) margarine or butter

3 tablespoons/45 mL granulated sugar

¼ teaspoon/1.25 mL ground cinnamon

1½ cups/350 mL crispy rice cereal

1 package (6 ounces/170 grams) diced dried mixed fruit (about 1⅓ cups/325 mL)

1 cup/250 mL **Quaker® 100% Whole Grain Large Flake Oats** or **Quaker® 100% Whole Grain Quick Oats** (uncooked)

Heat honey, margarine, sugar and cinnamon in medium saucepan over medium-low heat until margarine is melted, stirring frequently. Bring to a boil; cook 1 minute, stirring constantly. Remove from heat. Stir in rice cereal, dried fruit and oats until evenly coated.

Press mixture evenly onto bottom of ungreased 8-inch square baking pan. Cool completely. Cut into bars. Store tightly covered in refrigerator.

MAKES 16 BARS

FROZEN
BANANA
POPS

1¾ cups/450 mL **Quaker® Life® Original Cereal**

4 large firm ripe bananas (about 1½ pounds/680 grams)

¾ cup/175 mL creamy, chunky or flavoured peanut butter

8 thin wooden craft sticks

Place cereal in large resealable plastic bag. Squeeze bag to remove air and seal. Crush cereal coarsely with rolling pin or palm of hand. Transfer cereal to large plate.

Peel and cut bananas in half crosswise. Gently push craft stick about 1½ inches into cut end of each banana half.

Spread 1½ tablespoons/22.5 mL peanut butter evenly onto banana; roll in cereal to cover completely. Place on waxed paper. Repeat with remaining peanut butter, bananas and cereal.

Freeze bananas 1 hour or until coating is firm. Transfer pops to large freezer-safe resealable plastic bag; freeze completely. Remove pops from freezer 10 minutes before serving.

MAKES 8 POPS

BANANA NUT
CARAMEL
CRUNCH

¼ cup/60 mL low fat whipped topping

2 **Quaker® Crispy Minis® Caramel Corn Flavour Large Rice Cakes**

1 medium banana, sliced

1 tablespoon/15 mL low fat caramel sauce

4 dry-roasted peanuts, chopped

Spread whipped topping over rice cakes. Place banana slices on top and drizzle with caramel sauce. Sprinkle with chopped peanuts.

MAKES 2 SERVINGS

HOLIDAY
POLKA DOT
BARS

1 cup/250 mL (2 sticks) butter, softened

1½ cups/350 mL firmly packed brown sugar

2 large eggs

1 teaspoon/5 mL vanilla extract

1⅔ cups/400 mL all-purpose flour

1 cup/250 mL **Quaker® 100% Whole Grain Large Flake Oats** or **Quaker® 100% Whole Grain Quick Oats** (uncooked)

1 teaspoon/5 mL baking powder

1 teaspoon/5 mL salt

1¾ cups/450 mL milk chocolate or semi-sweet chocolate chips

Candy-coated chocolate pieces in holiday colours, holiday sprinkles in holiday colours or coloured sugars

Heat oven to 375°F/190°C. Spray 15×10-inch jelly-roll pan with nonstick cooking spray.

Beat butter and brown sugar in large bowl with electric mixer until creamy. Add eggs and vanilla extract; beat well. Combine flour, oats, baking powder and salt. Add to creamed mixture; mix well. Spread evenly into prepared pan.

Bake 18 to 20 minutes or until golden brown. Remove pan to wire rack.

Sprinkle chocolate chips evenly over hot cookie in pan; let stand until softened, about 1 minute. Spread softened chocolate evenly over cookie with spatula or knife. Sprinkle with candy-coated chocolate pieces; press down lightly. Cool completely. Cut into bars.

MAKES 48 BARS

PB & J TREATS

2   cups/500 mL **Quaker® 100% Whole Grain Large Flake Oats** or **Quaker® 100% Whole Grain Quick Oats** (uncooked)

1½   cups/350 mL all-purpose flour

¾   cup/175 mL firmly packed light brown sugar

1   teaspoon/5 mL baking soda

½   cup/125 mL (1 stick) butter, melted

½   cup/125 mL creamy peanut butter

1   cup/250 mL seedless strawberry jam, Concord grape jam or apricot preserves

½   cup/125 mL coarsely chopped dry-roasted peanuts

Heat oven to 350°F/180°C. Line 9-inch square pan with aluminum foil so foil extends beyond edges of pan. Spray foil with nonstick cooking spray.

Combine oats, flour, brown sugar, baking soda, and melted butter in large bowl; mix well. Reserve 1 cup/250 mL mixture for topping. Add peanut butter to remaining mixture; blend well. Press peanut butter mixture evenly into bottom of prepared pan. Spread jam evenly over top. Combine peanuts with reserved topping mixture in small bowl. Sprinkle crumb mixture evenly over jam.

Bake 35 minutes or until golden brown and bubbly. Remove to wire rack. Cool completely. Refrigerate 1 to 2 hours until set. Cut into bars.

MAKES 16 BARS

COOKIE JAR FAVORITES

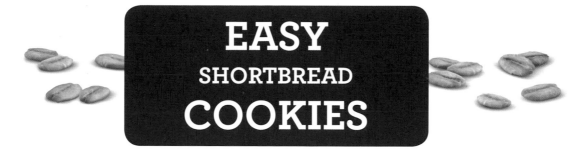

EASY
SHORTBREAD
COOKIES

1   cup/250 mL (2 sticks) margarine or butter, softened slightly

½   cup/125 mL granulated sugar

1   teaspoon/5 mL vanilla extract

2   cups/500 mL **Quaker® 100% Whole Grain Large Flake Oats** or **Quaker® 100% Whole Grain Quick Oats** (uncooked)

1¼ cups/300 mL all-purpose flour

    Coloured sugar or candy sprinkles

Heat oven to 350°F/180°C.

Place margarine in large (1-gallon/4-litre) resealable plastic bag. Squeeze with hands until very soft. Open bag; add sugar and vanilla extract. Reseal; squeeze and knead until ingredients are well mixed. Open bag; add oats and flour. Reseal; squeeze and knead until ingredients are well mixed. Open bag; scrape dough together with spatula and remove from bag.

Shape dough into 1-inch balls. Place on ungreased cookie sheets 2 inches apart; flatten with fingers or tines of fork to ¼-inch thickness. Decorate as desired with coloured sugar or candy sprinkles.

Bake 12 to 14 minutes or until bottoms are light golden brown. Cool 1 minute on cookie sheets; remove to wire racks. Cool completely. Store tightly covered.

MAKES ABOUT 24 COOKIES

COCONUT OATMEAL BISCOTTI

1 cup/250 mL **Quaker® 100% Whole Grain Large Flake Oats** or **Quaker® 100% Whole Grain Quick Oats** (uncooked)

1 cup/250 mL flaked sweetened coconut

½ cup/125 mL toasted chopped pecans

1¾ cups/450 mL all-purpose flour

¾ cup/175 mL firmly packed brown sugar

1½ teaspoons/7.5 mL baking powder

½ teaspoon/2.5 mL salt

¼ cup/60 mL light coconut milk

1 teaspoon/5 mL vanilla extract

2 large eggs

½ cup/125 mL white chocolate chips

Heat oven to 350°F/180°C. Line baking sheet with parchment paper.

Combine oats, coconut and pecans in food processor; process until finely ground. Lightly spoon flour into dry measuring cups; level with knife. Combine oat mixture, flour, brown sugar, baking powder and salt in large bowl; mix well. Combine coconut milk, vanilla extract and eggs in small bowl; mix well. Add to dry ingredients all at once; stir just until dry ingredients are moistened.

Turn dough out onto floured surface; knead lightly seven times with floured hands. Shape dough into 15×3-inch log on prepared baking sheet; pat to 1-inch thickness.

Bake 30 minutes. Remove to wire rack to cool.

Cut log diagonally into eighteen ½-inch slices. Place, cut sides down, on baking sheet. Reduce oven temperature to 325°F/160°C; bake 18 minutes. Turn cookies over; bake an additional 18 minutes. (Cookies will be slightly soft in centre but will harden as they cool.) Remove to wire rack to cool completely.

Place white chocolate chips in small microwave-safe bowl; microwave on HIGH 30 seconds or until almost melted, stirring until smooth. Spread evenly over tops of biscotti.

MAKES 18 BISCOTTI

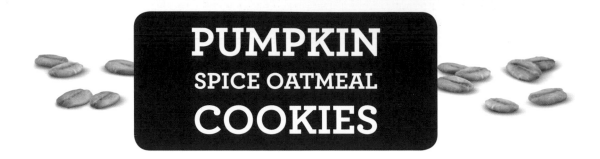

PUMPKIN
SPICE OATMEAL
COOKIES

COOKIES

- 1 cup/250 mL granulated sugar
- ½ cup/125 mL (1 stick) 70% vegetable oil spread
- 1 cup/250 mL canned pumpkin
- 2 egg whites or 1 egg
- 1 teaspoon/5 mL grated orange peel
- 2 cups/500 mL **Quaker® 100% Whole Grain Large Flake Oats or Quaker® 100% Whole Grain Quick Oats** (uncooked)
- 1 cup/250 mL all-purpose flour
- 1 teaspoon/5 mL pumpkin pie spice or ground cinnamon
- ½ teaspoon/2.5 mL baking soda
- ½ teaspoon/2.5 mL salt
- ½ cup/125 mL finely chopped pitted prunes
- ¼ cup/60 mL finely chopped walnuts

GLAZE

- ½ cup/125 mL powdered sugar
- 1 tablespoon/15 mL **Tropicana Pure Premium®** orange juice or **Dole®** 100% orange juice

Heat oven to 350°F/180°C. Lightly spray cookie sheets with nonstick cooking spray.

For cookies, beat granulated sugar and spread in large bowl with electric mixer until well blended. Add pumpkin, egg whites and orange peel; beat well. (Mixture will look curdled.) Add combined oats, flour, pumpkin pie spice, baking soda and salt; mix well. Stir in prunes and walnuts. Drop dough by rounded measuring tablespoonfuls/15 mL about 2 inches apart on cookie sheets.

Bake 11 to 13 minutes or until lightly browned. (Do not overbake. Centres of cookies will be soft.) Cool 1 minute on cookie sheets; remove to wire racks. Cool completely.

For glaze, combine powdered sugar and orange juice in small bowl; mix well. Drizzle glaze over cooled cookies. Let cookies stand until glaze sets. Store tightly covered.

MAKES ABOUT 48 COOKIES

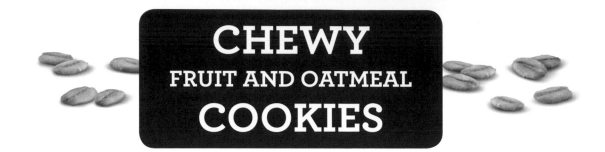

CHEWY
FRUIT AND OATMEAL
COOKIES

¾ cup/175 mL firmly packed brown sugar

½ cup/125 mL granulated sugar

1 container (8 ounces/225 grams) low fat vanilla or plain yogurt

2 large egg whites, lightly beaten

2 tablespoons/30 mL vegetable oil

2 tablespoons/30 mL fat-free (skim) milk

2 teaspoons/10 mL vanilla extract

1½ cups/350 mL all-purpose flour

1 teaspoon/5 mL baking soda

1 teaspoon/5 mL ground cinnamon

½ teaspoon/2.5 mL salt (optional)

3 cups/750 mL **Quaker® 100% Whole Grain Large Flake Oats** or **Quaker® 100% Whole Grain Quick Oats** (uncooked)

1 cup/250 mL diced dried mixed fruit, raisins or dried cranberries

Heat oven to 350°F/180°C.

Combine brown sugar, granulated sugar, yogurt, egg whites, oil, milk and vanilla extract in large bowl; mix well. Combine flour, baking soda, cinnamon and, if desired, salt in medium bowl; mix well. Add to yogurt mixture; mix well. Stir in oats and dried fruit. Drop dough by rounded tablespoonfuls/ 15 mL onto ungreased cookie sheets.

Bake 12 to 14 minutes or until light golden brown. Cool 1 minute on cookie sheets; remove to wire racks. Cool completely. Store loosely covered.

MAKES 36 COOKIES

OAT PECAN PRALINE COOKIES

1¼ cups/300 mL firmly packed brown sugar

1 cup/250 mL (2 sticks) margarine or butter, softened

2 eggs

2 tablespoons/30 mL molasses

1 teaspoon/5 mL maple extract

1¼ cups/300 mL all-purpose flour

1 teaspoon/5 mL baking soda

2½ cups/600 mL **Quaker® 100% Whole Grain Large Flake Oats** or **Quaker® 100% Whole Grain Quick Oats** (uncooked)

1 cup/250 mL pecans, coarsely chopped

¾ cup/175 mL pecan halves (about 48 halves)

Beat brown sugar and margarine in large bowl until creamy. Add eggs, molasses and maple extract; beat well. Add combined flour and baking soda; mix well. Add oats and chopped pecans; mix well. Cover; chill at least 1 hour.

Heat oven to 350°F/180°C. Lightly grease cookie sheets.

Shape dough into 1-inch balls. Place 3 inches apart on cookie sheets. Flatten each ball by pressing pecan half in centre.

Bake 10 to 12 minutes or until deep golden brown. Immediately remove from cookie sheets to wire racks. Cool completely. Store tightly covered.

MAKES ABOUT 48 COOKIES

OATMEAL
GINGERBREAD
COOKIES

1 cup/250 mL (2 sticks) margarine or butter, softened

¾ cup/175 mL firmly packed brown sugar

½ cup/125 mL molasses

1 egg

3⅓ cups/825 mL all-purpose flour

1½ cups/350 mL **Quaker® 100% Whole Grain Large Flake Oats or Quaker® 100% Whole Grain Quick Oats** (uncooked)

1 teaspoon/5 mL ground cinnamon

1 teaspoon/5 mL ground ginger

½ teaspoon/2.5 mL ground nutmeg

½ teaspoon/2.5 mL baking soda

¼ teaspoon/1.25 mL salt (optional)

Ready-to-spread frosting

Assorted candies

Beat margarine and brown sugar in large bowl until creamy. Add molasses and egg; beat well. Add combined flour, oats, cinnamon, ginger, nutmeg, baking soda and, if desired, salt; mix well. Cover; chill about 2 hours.

Heat oven to 350°F/180°C. On floured surface, roll dough out about ¼ inch thick for a chewy cookie or ⅛ inch thick for a crisp cookie. Cut with 5-inch gingerbread man or woman cookie cutter. Place on ungreased cookie sheets.

Bake 8 to 10 minutes or until set. Cool 1 minute on cookie sheets; remove to wire racks. Cool completely.

Frost and decorate cookies with candies. Store loosely covered at room temperature.

MAKES 20 (5-INCH) COOKIES

HONEY POT
OATMEAL
COOKIES

- 1 cup/250 mL honey
- 1 cup/250 mL peanut butter
- ¼ cup/60 mL granulated sugar
- ¼ cup/60 mL (½ stick) butter or margarine,* softened
- 1 egg, lightly beaten
- ¼ cup/60 mL milk
- 2 teaspoons/10 mL vanilla extract
- 3 cups/750 mL **Quaker® 100% Whole Grain Large Flake Oats** or **Quaker® 100% Whole Grain Quick Oats** (uncooked)
- 1¾ cups/450 mL all-purpose flour**
- 1 teaspoon/5 mL baking soda
- 1 cup/250 mL golden raisins
- ½ cup/125 mL coarsely chopped dry-roasted peanuts (optional)

Soft spreads in tubs and stick spreads with less than 70% vegetable oil are not recommended for this recipe.

**If using large flake oats, add 2 tablespoons/30 mL additional flour.*

Heat oven to 375°F/190°C.

Beat honey, peanut butter, sugar and butter in large bowl with electric mixer until creamy. Add egg, milk and vanilla extract; mix well. Add combined oats, flour and baking soda; mix well. Stir in raisins and, if desired, peanuts. Drop dough by rounded tablespoonfuls/15 mL onto ungreased cookie sheets.

Bake 7 to 10 minutes or until light golden brown. Remove to wire racks; cool completely. Store tightly covered at room temperature or wrap airtight and freeze.

MAKES ABOUT 60 COOKIES

OATMEAL MACAROONS

1 cup/250 mL (2 sticks) margarine or butter, softened

1 cup/250 mL firmly packed brown sugar

2 eggs

½ teaspoon/2.5 mL almond extract

1¼ cups/300 mL all-purpose flour

1 teaspoon/5 mL baking soda

3 cups/750 mL **Quaker® 100% Whole Grain Large Flake Oats or Quaker® 100% Whole Grain Quick Oats** (uncooked)

1 package (4 ounces/120 grams) flaked or shredded coconut (about 1⅓ cups/325 mL)

Heat oven to 350°F/180°C. Lightly grease cookie sheets.

Beat margarine and brown sugar in large bowl with electric mixer until creamy. Add eggs and almond extract; beat well. Add combined flour and baking soda; mix well. Add oats and coconut; mix well.

Drop dough by rounded teaspoonfuls/5 mL onto prepared cookie sheets.

Bake 8 to 10 minutes or until light golden brown. Cool 2 minutes on cookie sheets; remove to wire racks. Cool completely. Store tightly covered.

MAKES 48 COOKIES

COCOA OATMEAL COOKIES

1 cup/250 mL (2 sticks) butter or margarine, softened

1 cup/250 mL firmly packed brown sugar

½ cup/125 mL granulated sugar

2 large eggs

1 teaspoon/5 mL vanilla extract

1½ cups/350 mL all-purpose flour

⅓ cup/75 mL unsweetened cocoa powder

1 teaspoon/5 mL baking soda

1 teaspoon/5 mL salt (optional)

3 cups/750 mL **Quaker® 100% Whole Grain Large Flake Oats** or **Quaker® 100% Whole Grain Quick Oats** (uncooked)

1 cup/250 mL raisins (optional)

Heat oven to 375°F/190°C.

Beat butter, brown sugar and granulated sugar until creamy. Add eggs and vanilla extract; beat well. Add combined flour, cocoa, baking soda and, if desired, salt; mix well. Stir in oats and, if desired, raisins; mix well. Drop dough by rounded tablespoonfuls/15 mL onto ungreased cookie sheets.

Bake 10 to 12 minutes or until cookies are almost set. (Do not overbake.) Cool 1 minute on cookie sheets; remove to wire racks. Cool completely. Store tightly covered.

MAKES 48 COOKIES

PEANUT
BUTTER CUP
COOKIES

1½ cups/350 mL firmly packed brown sugar

1 cup/250 mL (2 sticks) margarine or butter, softened

¾ cup/175 mL peanut butter (not reduced-fat)

2 eggs

2 teaspoons/10 mL vanilla extract

1½ cups/350 mL all-purpose flour

⅓ cup/75 mL unsweetened cocoa powder

1 teaspoon/5 mL baking soda

¼ teaspoon/1.25 mL salt (optional)

2 cups/500 mL **Quaker® 100% Whole Grain Large Flake Oats or Quaker® 100% Whole Grain Quick Oats** (uncooked)

1 package (9 ounces/255 grams) mini peanut butter cup candies, unwrapped, cut into halves or quarters (about 35 candies)

Heat oven to 350°F/180°C. Beat brown sugar, margarine and peanut butter until creamy. Add eggs and vanilla extract; beat well. Combine flour, cocoa, baking soda and, if desired, salt in small bowl; mix well. Add to creamed mixture; mix well. Stir in oats and candy; mix well.

Drop dough by level ¼-cup/60-mL portions 3 inches apart onto ungreased cookie sheets.

Bake 12 to 14 minutes or until cookies are slightly firm to the touch. (Do not overbake.) Cool 1 minute on cookie sheets; remove to wire racks. Cool completely. Store tightly covered.

MAKES 36 COOKIES

OATMEAL BUTTER BRITTLE COOKIES

2 cups/500 mL **Quaker® 100% Whole Grain Large Flake Oats** or **Quaker® 100% Whole Grain Quick Oats** (uncooked)

1¼ cups/300 mL all-purpose flour

½ teaspoon/2.5 mL baking powder

1 cup/250 mL (2 sticks) butter or margarine, chilled and cut into pieces

1 cup/250 mL powdered sugar

⅔ cup/150 mL firmly packed brown sugar

1½ tablespoons/22.5 mL water

1 teaspoon/5 mL vanilla extract

1 cup/250 mL chopped dry-roasted or lightly salted peanuts

2 cups/500 mL (12 ounces/360 grams) semi-sweet chocolate chips, divided

Heat oven to 350°F/180°C. Line two cookie sheets with aluminum foil.

Combine oats, flour and baking powder in large bowl; mix well. Add butter. Beat with electric mixer at low to medium speed until crumbly. Add powdered sugar, brown sugar, water and vanilla extract. Beat at low speed until dough starts to form. Stir in peanuts by hand.

Divide dough in half. Place one half on one cookie sheet; flatten with lightly floured hands into 13×9-inch rectangle. Repeat using remaining dough and second cookie sheet.

Bake 22 to 25 minutes or until golden brown, rotating cookie sheets after 12 minutes. Place cookie sheets on wire racks.

Sprinkle 1 cup/250 mL chocolate chips evenly over each large cookie. Let stand 2 to 3 minutes. With spatula or knife, spread softened chocolate evenly over cookies. Cool completely. (Refrigerate 15 minutes to set chocolate, if necessary.)

Remove large cookies from cookie sheets and peel off foil. Break each into 24 pieces. Store tightly covered in cool place.

MAKES 48 COOKIES

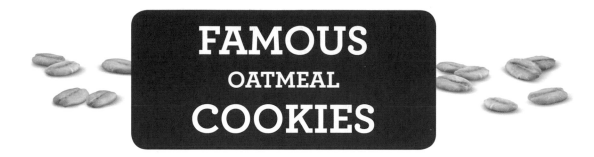

- 1 cup/250 mL firmly packed brown sugar
- ¾ cup/175 mL vegetable shortening
- ½ cup/125 mL granulated sugar
- 1 egg
- ¼ cup/60 mL water
- 1 teaspoon/5 mL vanilla extract
- 3 cups/750 mL **Quaker® 100% Whole Grain Large Flake Oats** or **Quaker® 100% Whole Grain Quick Oats** (uncooked)
- 1 cup/250 mL all-purpose flour
- 1 teaspoon/5 mL salt (optional)
- ½ teaspoon/2.5 mL baking soda

Heat oven to 350°F/180°C.

Beat brown sugar, shortening and granulated sugar in large bowl until creamy. Add egg, water and vanilla extract; beat well. Add combined oats, flour, salt, if desired, and baking soda; mix well. Drop dough by rounded teaspoonfuls/5 mL onto ungreased cookie sheets.

Bake 11 to 13 minutes or until edges are golden brown. Remove to wire racks. Cool completely. Store tightly covered.

MAKES ABOUT 60 COOKIES

HIGH ALTITUDE ADJUSTMENT: Increase flour to 1¼ cups/300 mL and bake as directed.

VARIATIONS:
- Add 1 cup/250 mL of any one or a combination of any of the following ingredients to basic cookie dough: raisins, chopped nuts, chocolate chips or shredded coconut.
- For large cookies, drop by rounded tablespoonfuls/15 mL onto ungreased cookie sheets. Bake 15 to 17 minutes.
- For bar cookies, press dough onto bottom of ungreased 13×9-inch baking pan. Bake 30 to 35 minutes or until light golden brown. Cool completely in pan on wire rack. Cut into bars. Store tightly covered. Makes 24 bars.

CANDY CANE COOKIES

¾ cup/175 mL (1½ sticks) butter or margarine

1 cup/250 mL granulated sugar

1 egg

½ teaspoon/2.5 mL vanilla extract

¼ teaspoon/1.25 mL peppermint extract

2 cups/500 mL sifted all-purpose flour

½ teaspoon/2.5 mL baking powder

¼ teaspoon/1.25 mL salt

1 cup/250 mL **Quaker® 100% Whole Grain Large Flake Oats** or **Quaker® 100% Whole Grain Quick Oats** (uncooked)

Heat oven to 375°F/190°C.

Beat butter and sugar until creamy. Blend in egg, vanilla extract and peppermint extract. Sift together flour, baking powder and salt; gradually add to creamed mixture. Stir in oats. Roll out dough between two sheets of waxed paper to form 12×6-inch rectangle. Refrigerate several hours or overnight.

Remove top sheet of waxed paper. Cut into 6×¼-inch slices. Shape into ropes, twisting to form candy canes. Place on ungreased cookie sheets.

Bake 8 to 10 minutes or until set. Cool 1 minute on cookie sheets; remove to wire racks.

Decorate with powdered sugar frosting and red hot cinnamon candies.

MAKES 48 COOKIES

PEPPERMINT SUGAR TOPPING: Crush 12 round hard peppermint candies (or 6 small candy canes) in blender. Transfer to small bowl. Add 3 tablespoons/45 mL granulated sugar; mix well. Sprinkle on top of cookies immediately after removing cookie sheets from oven.

SNOWMAN COOKIES: Eliminate peppermint extract. After twisting dough into ropes, shape each rope into a circle, pinching ends to seal. Stack three circles on top of one another on cookie sheet forming snowmen. Bake according to directions, increasing time by 2 to 3 minutes if needed. Transfer cookies to wire racks; sprinkle with powdered sugar while warm. Cool completely.

SPARKLING
SNOWFLAKE
COOKIES

1   package (18.25 ounces/515 grams) white cake mix

1   cup/250 mL (2 sticks) butter or margarine, softened

1   egg

1   teaspoon/5 mL vanilla extract

2   cups/500 mL **Quaker® 100% Whole Grain Large Flake Oats** or **Quaker® 100% Whole Grain Quick Oats** (uncooked)

Assorted coloured sugars, candy sprinkles, small candies or decorator icings (optional)

Heat oven to 350°F/180°C. Combine half of cake mix, butter, egg and vanilla extract in large bowl; mix thoroughly. Stir in remaining cake mix and oats; mix well.

Divide dough in half. On well-floured surface, using well-floured rolling pin, roll each half no more than ¼ inch thick. Cut dough with 3-inch snowflake or other large holiday cookie cutter. Place about 1 inch apart on ungreased cookie sheets. If cookies will be used as tree ornaments, poke hole at top of each cookie with drinking straw before baking. (Repeat immediately after baking if hole closes.)

Bake 6 to 8 minutes or just until set (centres may still be soft). Carefully remove to wire racks; cool completely. Decorate, if desired.

MAKES 30 COOKIES

DECORATING IDEAS:
• Sprinkle with coloured sugars, candy sprinkles or small candies before baking.
• Sprinkle baked cookies with powdered sugar as they cool.
• Frost cooled cookies with homemade or ready-to-spread frosting. Sprinkle with edible glitter or coloured sugar.
• Squeeze melted dark or white chocolate, decorator frosting or decorator gel in tubes onto cooled cookies.

tip

Dragées (small silver and gold ball-shaped decorations) are inedible and should only be placed on cookies that will be used for decorations and not eaten.

HOLIDAY
OATMEAL COOKIE
BRITTLE

2 cups/500 mL **Quaker® 100% Whole Grain Large Flake Oats** or **Quaker® 100% Whole Grain Quick Oats** (uncooked)

1½ cups/350 mL all-purpose flour

½ teaspoon/2.5 mL baking powder

1 cup/250 mL (2 sticks) cold butter, cut into small pieces

1 cup/250 mL powdered sugar

⅔ cup/150 mL firmly packed brown sugar

1½ teaspoons/7.5 mL water

1 teaspoon/5 mL vanilla extract

2 cups/500 mL (12-ounce/360-gram package) bittersweet or semi-sweet chocolate chips

⅔ cup/150 mL white chocolate chips

Edible gold dust (optional)

Heat oven to 350°F/180°C. Line two large cookie sheets with aluminum foil.

Combine oats, flour and baking powder in large bowl; mix well. Add butter. Beat with electric mixer at low to medium speed until crumbly. Add powdered sugar, brown sugar, water and vanilla extract. Beat at low speed until dough forms.

Divide dough in half. Place one half on one cookie sheet; flatten with lightly floured hands into 13×9-inch rectangle, about ⅛ inch thick. Repeat using remaining dough and second cookie sheet.

Bake 22 to 25 minutes or until golden brown, rotating cookie sheets after 12 minutes. Remove cookie sheets to wire racks.

Sprinkle 1 cup/250 mL chocolate chips evenly over each large warm cookie. Let stand 2 to 3 minutes. Spread softened chocolate evenly over cookies with spatula or knife. Sprinkle white chocolate chips evenly over smooth chocolate on both cookies; let stand 2 to 3 minutes. Run through white chocolate with tip of knife, dragging it into dark chocolate, making marble-like streaks. Sprinkle with gold dust, if desired. Cool completely. (Refrigerate 15 minutes to set chocolate, if necessary.)

Remove large cookies from cookie sheets and peel off foil. Break each into 24 pieces. Store tightly covered in cool place.

tip

Edible gold dust can be found at specialty baking stores.

MAKES 48 COOKIES

APPLE
OATMEAL SPICE
COOKIES

1½ cups/350 mL all-purpose flour

1 teaspoon/5 mL baking soda

1 teaspoon/5 mL ground cinnamon

½ teaspoon/2.5 mL salt (optional)

¼ teaspoon/1.25 mL ground nutmeg (optional)

¾ cup/175 mL firmly packed brown sugar

½ cup/125 mL granulated sugar

¼ cup/60 mL (½ stick) margarine, softened

¾ cup/175 mL apple butter or applesauce

2 egg whites or 1 egg

2 tablespoons/30 mL fat-free (skim) milk

2 teaspoons/10 mL vanilla extract

3 cups/750 mL **Quaker® 100% Whole Grain Large Flake Oats** or **Quaker® 100% Whole Grain Quick Oats** (uncooked)

1 cup/250 mL diced dried mixed fruit or raisins

Heat oven to 350°F/180°C. Lightly spray cookie sheets with nonstick cooking spray.

Combine flour, baking soda, cinnamon and, if desired, salt and nutmeg in medium bowl; mix well. Beat brown sugar, granulated sugar and margarine in large bowl with electric mixer until well blended. Add apple butter, egg whites, milk and vanilla extract; beat well. Stir in dry ingredients; mix well. Stir in oats and dried fruit; mix well. (Dough will be moist.)

Drop dough by rounded tablespoonfuls/15 mL onto prepared cookie sheets.

Bake 10 to 12 minutes or until edges are light golden brown. Cool 1 minute on cookie sheets; remove to wire racks. Cool completely. Store tightly covered.

MAKES 36 COOKIES

tip

Look for apple butter in the jam and jelly section of the supermarket.

RUDOLPH'S
CARROT CAKE
COOKIES

COOKIES

1 cup/250 mL (2 sticks) butter, softened

⅔ cup/150 mL firmly packed brown sugar

1 large egg

¼ cup/60 mL molasses

2 tablespoons/30 mL milk

1 teaspoon/5 mL vanilla extract

1½ cups/350 mL all-purpose flour

½ teaspoon/2.5 mL baking soda

½ teaspoon/2.5 mL ground allspice or ground cinnamon

2 cups/500 mL **Quaker® 100% Whole Grain Large Flake Oats** or **Quaker® 100% Whole Grain Quick Oats** (uncooked)

1 cup/250 mL grated carrots

½ cup/125 mL raisins

GLAZE

1 cup/250 mL powdered sugar

3 to 4 teaspoons/15 to 20 mL milk

½ teaspoon/2.5 mL vanilla extract

Heat oven to 375°F/190°C.

For cookies, beat butter and brown sugar in large bowl until creamy. Add egg, molasses, milk and vanilla extract; beat well. Combine flour, baking soda and allspice in medium bowl; mix well. Add to creamed mixture; mix well. Stir in oats, carrots and raisins; mix well. Drop by rounded tablespoonfuls/15 mL onto ungreased cookie sheets.

Bake 10 to 12 minutes or until light golden brown. Cool 1 minute on cookie sheets; remove to wire racks. Cool completely.

For glaze, combine all ingredients; mix well. Drizzle over cookies. Let glaze set. Store in tightly covered container.

MAKES 36 COOKIES

OATMEAL SCOTCHIES

1 cup/250 mL (2 sticks) margarine or butter, softened

¾ cup/175 mL granulated sugar

¾ cup/175 mL firmly packed brown sugar

2 eggs

1 teaspoon/5 mL vanilla extract

1¼ cups/300 mL all-purpose flour

1 teaspoon/5 mL baking soda

½ teaspoon/2.5 mL salt (optional)

3 cups/750 mL **Quaker® 100% Whole Grain Large Flake Oats** or **Quaker® 100% Whole Grain Quick Oats** (uncooked)

2 cups/500 mL (12-ounce/360-gram package) butterscotch chips

Heat oven to 375°F/190°C. Beat margarine, granulated sugar and brown sugar in large bowl until creamy. Add eggs and vanilla extract; beat well. Combine flour, baking soda and, if desired, salt in small bowl; mix well. Add to creamed mixture; mix well. Add oats and butterscotch chips; mix well.

Drop dough by level tablespoons/15 mL onto ungreased cookie sheets.

Bake 7 to 8 minutes for chewy cookies or 9 to 10 minutes for crisp cookies. Cool 2 minutes on cookie sheets. Transfer to wire racks; cool completely. Store tightly covered.

MAKES 48 COOKIES

SANTA SANDWICH COOKIES

- 1 cup/250 mL (2 sticks) butter or margarine, softened
- 1 cup/250 mL granulated sugar
- 1 teaspoon/5 mL vanilla extract
- 1¾ cups/450 mL all-purpose flour
- 1 cup/250 mL **Quaker® 100% Whole Grain Large Flake Oats** or **Quaker® 100% Whole Grain Quick Oats** (uncooked)
- ¼ teaspoon/1.25 mL salt
- 1 container (16 ounces/454 grams) ready-to-spread vanilla-flavoured frosting

  Green or red food colouring (optional)

  Coloured sugars and holiday sprinkles

Beat butter, sugar and vanilla extract in large bowl with electric mixer until creamy. Combine flour, oats and salt in medium bowl; mix well. Add to creamed mixture; mix well. Divide dough in half. Shape each half into 2-inch diameter roll (approximately 5 inches long). Wrap in plastic wrap; chill about 3 hours or longer.

Heat oven to 350°F/180°C. Unwrap one roll of dough and cut into ¼-inch slices. Place slices about 1 inch apart on ungreased cookie sheets. Repeat with remaining roll.

Bake 12 to 14 minutes or until edges are light golden brown. Cool 1 minute on cookie sheets; remove to wire racks. Cool completely.

Divide frosting in half. Cover and refrigerate half of frosting for another use. Tint remaining frosting with food colouring, if desired. Spread frosting on bottom of one cooled cookie; top with second cookie. Roll edge of frosting in decorations. Repeat with remaining cookies. Store tightly covered.

MAKES 24 SANDWICH COOKIES

PEANUTTY
CHOCO-CHERRY
NO-BAKE TREATS

1 cup/250 mL peanut butter-chocolate spread

¾ cup/175 mL powdered sugar

4 to 6 tablespoons/60 to 90 mL milk or water, divided

2 cups/500 mL **Quaker® 100% Whole Grain Large Flake Oats** or **Quaker® 100% Whole Grain Quick Oats** (uncooked)

⅓ cup/75 mL coarsely chopped dry-roasted peanuts

1 cup/250 mL golden raisin/dried cherry fruit mix

Combine peanut butter-chocolate spread, powdered sugar and 4 tablespoons/60 mL milk in large bowl; mix well. Stir in oats, peanuts and dried fruit; mix well. Add additional milk if needed.

Drop by rounded teaspoonfuls/5 mL onto waxed paper. Let stand 1 to 2 hours or until set. Store in tightly covered container.

MAKES 48 TREATS

tip

If raisin/dried cherry fruit mix is not available, substitute ½ cup/ 125 mL each golden raisins and dried cherries or dried cranberries.

INDEX

METRIC CONVERSION CHART

VOLUME MEASUREMENTS (DRY)

⅛ teaspoon	=	0.625 mL (millilitre)
¼ teaspoon	=	1.25 mL
½ teaspoon	=	2.5 mL
¾ teaspoon	=	3.75 mL
1 teaspoon	=	5 mL
1 tablespoon	=	15 mL
¼ cup	=	60 mL
⅓ cup	=	75 mL
½ cup	=	125 mL
⅔ cup	=	150 mL
¾ cup	=	175 mL
1 cup	=	250 mL
1⅛ cups	=	275 mL
1¼ cups	=	300 mL
1⅓ cups	=	325 mL
1½ cups	=	350 mL
1⅔ cups	=	400 mL
1¾ cups	=	450 mL
2 cups	=	500 mL
2½ cups	=	600 mL
3 cups	=	750 mL
3⅔ cups	=	900 mL
4 cups	=	1 quart = 1 litre

VOLUME MEASUREMENTS (FLUID)

1 fluid ounce (2 tablespoons)	=	30 mL
4 fluid ounces (½ cup)	=	125 mL
8 fluid ounces (1 cup)	=	250 mL
12 fluid ounces (1½ cups)	=	375 mL
16 fluid ounces (2 cups)	=	500 mL

DIMENSIONS

1⁄16 inch	=	2 mm
⅛ inch	=	3 mm
¼ inch	=	6 mm
½ inch	=	1.5 cm
¾ inch	=	2 cm
1 inch	=	2.5 cm

OVEN TEMPERATURES

250°F	=	120°C
275°F	=	140°C
300°F	=	150°C
325°F	=	160°C
350°F	=	180°C
375°F	=	190°C
400°F	=	200°C
425°F	=	220°C
450°F	=	230°C

WEIGHTS (MASS)

½ ounce	=	15 grams
1 ounce	=	30 grams
3 ounces	=	90 grams
4 ounces	=	120 grams
6 ounces	=	170 grams
8 ounces	=	225 grams
10 ounces	=	285 grams
12 ounces	=	360 grams
16 ounces	=	454 grams = 1 pound

BAKING PAN SIZES

Utensil	Size in Inches or Quarts	Metric Volume	Size in Centimeters
Baking Pan or Cake Pan (square or rectangular)	8×8×2 9×9×2 12×8×2 13×9×2	2 litres 2.5 litres 3 litres 3.5 litres	20×20×5 23×23×5 30×20×5 33×23×5
Loaf Pan	8×4×3 9×5×3	1.5 litres 2 litres	20×10×7 23×13×7
Round Layer Cake Pan	8×1½ 9×1½	1.2 litres 1.5 litres	20×4 23×4
Pie Plate	8×1¼ 9×1¼	750 mL 1 litre	20×3 23×3
Baking Dish or Casserole	1 quart 1½ quarts 2 quarts	1 litre 1.5 litres 2 litres	— — —